The Greening of
the European Union?

Contemporary European Studies, 14

The Greening of
the European Union?

Examining the EU's Environmental Credentials

Jon Burchell
and Simon Lightfoot

★ UACES ★

SHEFFIELD ACADEMIC PRESS
A Continuum imprint
LONDON • NEW YORK

Published by Sheffield Academic Press Ltd
The Tower Building, 11 York Road, London SE1 7NX
370 Lexington Avenue, New York NY 10017-6550

www.SheffieldAcademicPress.com
www.continuumbooks.com

British Library Cataloguing-in-Publication Data

A catalogue record for this book is available from the British Library

Typeset by Sheffield Academic Press
Printed on acid-free paper in Great Britain by MPG Books Ltd, Bodmin, Cornwall

ISBN 1-84127-275-2 (paperback)
      1-84127-317-1 (hardback)

Contents

Tables

Series Foreword

This is the fourteenth commissioned book in the Contemporary European Studies series resulting from collaboration between the University Association of Contemporary European Studies (UACES) and Sheffield Academic Press. It is also the first since I assumed the responsibility of series editor from Clive Archer, following his election as Chair of UACES. Thanks to his enthusiasm, commitment, and sheer hard work, the series has established itself in just three years as a major source of accessible but authoritative analysis of key events and issues in contemporary Europe. UACES and the editorial board owe him a great debt and it will be my challenge as the new editor to ensure that the series continues to attract high calibre authors and to address the topics that are important to those who are studying and teaching European studies or who have a professional interest in current developments.

Clearly the environment is one of the most important public policy issues today and the Eurobarometer public opinion polls suggest that there is very widespread acceptance that it is one of the areas where the EU should play an active role. In early 2001 the EU launched its Sixth Environmental Action Programme with the grandiose title 'Our Future, our Choice'. This book therefore provides a timely critical analysis of the extent to which there has indeed been a 'greening' of the EU and sets the development of the EU's environmental policy within the wider context of the debates surrounding green politics.

The professional skills and support of Heidi Robbins and Audrey Mann at Sheffield Academic Press have been very much appreciated in ensuring that the book has been produced speedily and efficiently.

Jackie Gower
Series Editor

Acknowledgments

The preparation and writing of this book have involved the support of various people and organizations. We would particularly like to thank Jackie Gower for her useful suggestions and advice on the text. Additionally, David Phinnemore, Mike Mannin and Liz Sperling provided us with helpful comments on the text. Our colleagues at Liverpool John Moores University have provided encouragement during the production of the book. Both authors would especially like to thank Professor Larry Wilde of Nottingham Trent University for his long-standing encouragement and friendship. Heidi Robbins, Elaine Bingham and everyone at Sheffield Academic Press did a professional job in converting our manuscript into the finished product. This book would not have got off the ground were it not for delays on the Liverpool–Sheffield line, so Central Trains must get a mention! Finally, thanks to Joe and Sam, for their support and patience over the years.

Abbreviations

CAP	Common Agricultural Policy
CEC	Commission of the European Communities
CNE	Climate Network Europe
DG	Directorate General
EAP	Environmental Action Programme
EEA	European Environmental Agency
EEB	European Environmental Bureau
EEC	European Economic Community
EC	European Community
ECJ	European Court of Justice
ECPS	Environment and Consumer Protection Service
EFA	European Free Alliance
EP	European Parliament
EPP	European People's Party
EU	European Union
FoE	Friends of the Earth
GGEP	Green Group in the European Parliament
IFN	International Friends of Nature
IGC	Intergovernmental Conference
MEP	Member of the European Parliament
NGO	non-governmental organization
QMV	qualified majority voting
SEA	Single European Act
SMEs	small and medium-sized enterprises
T&E	European Federation for Transport and Environment
TEU	Treaty on European Union
UN	United Nations
WWF	World Wide Fund for Nature

1 |

Introduction

Since the 1980s environmentalists have consistently argued for international action in the fight against environmental destruction. The broad repercussions of environmental disasters, such as the Chernobyl explosion and emerging debates surrounding global warming and the expanding hole in the ozone layer, have highlighted the inadequacy of seeking to tackle environmental issues at the national level. If environmental damage does not stop at national borders, it is argued, why should the policies seeking to prevent it? Given the global nature of environmental problems, there is a strong case to suggest that these can only be confronted effectively through the harmonization of environmental attitudes and legislation, and through the search for international solutions which extend beyond strictly national priorities and concerns.

The European Union (EU)[1] by its very nature and rationale, has become a prime focus as a potential initiator for environmental action within Europe. At the heart of the EU's growth and development has been the drive towards greater integration of policy and action across member states. While this has predominantly focused upon collective economic development, the emergence of broad-based international policy agreements and the emphasis upon collective action undoubtedly provides the potential for a framework within which the environmental approach outlined above could evolve.

A brief glance at recent EU environmental policy development would appear to suggest that this potential might be in the process of being realized. The EU has, it seems, taken to its role as a potential environmental 'guardian' with increasing commitment and enthusiasm. At the Earth Summit in 1992, the European Community (EC) was the only non-governmental signatory. More recently, the introduction of the sixth

---

1. As is the academic norm, we use the term European Union throughout except where referring to a period or an issue which applies directly to the European Community.

environmental action programme (EAP) was intended to be a significant step in the transition towards a more sustainable pattern of development within Europe, building upon the successes of the fifth EAP.

The growth in significance of the EU within the environmental sphere is also evident in the expanding number of green actors at this level. In recent years the EU has represented an important focal point for the continued development of both environmental non-governmental organizations (NGOs) and European green parties. Environmental movements, in seeking to influence the shape of European environmental policy and holding national governments to account for environmentally damaging actions and processes, have increasingly devoted significant energy to utilizing EU channels. In addition, direct elections to the European Parliament (EP) have enabled a number of European green parties to gain their first experiences of parliamentary representation, as well as shaping a vociferous green voice within the EP. Following the 1999 European Parliamentary elections, the Green Group in the European Parliament (GGEP) constituted 6% of the parliamentary members, and contained representatives from 11 EU member states. As the EP has grown in stature and influence over recent years, so too has the impact of the green dimension within it.

The image of the EU as 'environmental protector', however, is not necessarily as clear-cut as these portraits suggest. Indeed there is strong evidence for a counter argument which proposes that the very rationale for the EU itself represents a major factor in contributing towards increasing environmental problems within Europe, rather than providing effective solutions. How can the EU deal effectively with environmental problems when arguably the underlying cause of many of these problems has been the pattern of continuous economic growth and industrial development, upon which the EU has focused? There is, therefore, evidence to suggest that the EU may be represented as both a key factor in identifying the source of modern environmental problems and, conversely, a primary focal point through which to instigate potential environmental solutions.

This book critically examines the EU's developing relationship with the green agenda in an attempt to identify links between the emerging pattern of green politics and the patterns of policy making within the EU. It examines why and how the environment has become such a significant part of the EU's activities and assesses the extent of the 'greening' of the Union. It does not provide a detailed examination of all aspects in the development of environmental policy within the EU, although these issues are obviously discussed throughout. Rather, the book attempts to present a broader perspective that highlights the changing influence of green ideas and issues upon the evolution of the EU. In particular, how, and to what extent, has green politics impacted upon the EU institutions, its other policies and its progress towards sustainability? In tackling these questions, the book assesses the progress of the EU's environmental dimension largely from a green standpoint and questions whether these aims can be effectively instigated given the underlying economic rationale that has arguably been the driving force behind the EU's development so far.

When tackling these questions, however, there is the challenge that the EU institutions represent a far from homogeneous body of organizations. As such, green politics must seek to infiltrate and gain influence through various diverse channels. To illustrate the variety of the channels available, this book employs the template devised by Peterson and Bomberg (1999) to understand EU decision making. They identify three main types of decision-making rules: history-making, policy-setting and policy-shaping. These templates provide a useful guide to the different roles played by the institutions and the manner in which they interact. Given this diversity among the different EU institutions, an assessment of the greening of the EU requires an equally broad-ranging approach. The book therefore examines the extent to which green discourse within the EU has evolved as the scope of environmental policy and the influence of green actors has increased. In short, can the EU provide an effective channel for green politics?

To construct this picture of green politics in the EU, the book highlights a number of different dimensions, providing a comprehensive overview of the issues and themes surrounding the 'greening' of the EU. First, it examines the theoretical links between the ideas and concepts underlying EU development and those at the heart of green political theory. Secondly, it traces the emergence of environmental policy and assesses the priorities and direction in which green policy making within the EU is progressing. Thirdly, the book investigates the opportunities that the EU provides for green movements and parties to shape the political agendas at both EU and national levels. It also discusses the 'green critique' of the EU as a decision-making body.

By examining the relationship between the EU and the environment along these different dimensions, the book aims to provide a broad and comprehensive picture of the status of green issues within the Union, as well as a clear and informative guide to the debates surrounding this emerging aspect of EU activity. It is argued that the EU has progressed significantly within the environmental policy field, and in doing so has incorporated a much wider notion of green discourse and ideas. Its core policies, however, in particular its perception of a sustainable society, remain largely wedded to a discourse of ecological modernization rather than the more ambitious ecological discourse and objectives advocated by environmental theorists, European green parties and environmental pressure groups. In addition, it argues that there is a lack of coherence regarding the application of the concept of sustainability when it is applied to EU policy. This book argues that an increasing recognition of environmental issues may also raise some challenging questions regarding the democratic and structural nature of the EU itself.

Our starting point for this analysis traces the emergence of a new green politics and the concepts and ideas that have developed from this. Chapter 2 provides an overview of the environmental tradition and green political theory. By identifying the primary responses to under-standing environmental problems, the chapter demonstrates why it is possible to identify the EU as both a potential focal point for effective environmental policy making but also an ecological threat itself. The chapter also demonstrates the broad conception of the environmental problem and highlights different perceptions of what is entailed in developing a solution. It examines the importance of international cooperation and legislation as a vital feature of future environmental protection programmes and the creation of environmental standards.

Having identified the potential for action at the EU level, Chapter 3 looks at how the EU has transformed this potential into actual policy, tracing the development of environmental policy making within the EU. Although no explicit provision was made for the development of environmental policy within the Treaty of Rome, the chapter demon-strates how, through an effective interpretation of Articles 94 (100) and 308 (235),[2] the EU gained a tentative constitutional basis for environ-mental action, which has blossomed to such an extent that the environment had become one of the fastest growing areas of EU policy making. Overall, the chapter argues that the development of EU

---

2.   The Treaty articles were renumbered as a result of the Treaty of Amsterdam. The new article numbers are used throughout, although for the most important articles the old article numbers are included in parentheses.

environmental policy has been characterized by a steady expansion of EU competence within this field. It examines why formal legal competence was included in the Single European Act (SEA), before explaining how EU environmental policy has developed under the Maastricht and Amsterdam Treaties. This analysis will include a brief outline of the formal mechanisms for making environmental policy post-Nice. In particular, it focuses upon the principles and objectives of EU environmental policy and EU decision making. In doing so, it highlights the diverse stances of member states over the development of environmental standards and legislation.

As EU environmental policy has expanded, so inevitably has the number of movements and actors seeking to influence and shape this policy-making process. The growth and role of these actors provides the focus for Chapter 4. In particular, the chapter concentrates upon the emerging role for green organizations and parties, placing the political opportunities and activities of the green actors within the broader context of interest group competition within the EU. The chapter examines the channels through which the green lobby has attempted to gain an influential voice at EU level. It focuses upon the broad environmental network active at EU level, identifying the key actors and assessing the extent to which these groups have successfully adapted to lobbying at EU level.

Three key channels are examined in depth; namely the lobbying role of environmental movements, the parliamentary role of the GGEP, and the emerging, and potentially influential, role of the European Environmental Agency (EEA). As well as examining the work of those actors established in Brussels, the chapter also reflects upon the role of the national environmental movements. The chapter identifies some of the primary barriers and debates that pose significant problems for the effective coordination of environmental interests at EU level.

Chapter 5 assesses the impact of both green politics and green pressure within the EU, via an examination of one of the centrepieces of contemporary EU environmental policy: the environmental action programmes. Having traced the development of the first four programmes, the chapter assesses the impact and implementation of the fifth EAP. The fifth EAP was said to represent a significant development as it introduced the concept of 'sustainable development' into the EU's environmental policy-making agenda. It investigates the EU's approach to the concept of sustainable development, comparing sustainable development in broad ecological terms with the strategy of the fifth EAP to assess how the EU has adopted the concept. The chapter will, therefore, consider the concept of sustainable development in broad ecological terms and compare this perception to the definition, and subsequent strategy, offered within the fifth EAP. To do this, the chapter will examine the key 'target sectors' highlighted by the programme, (industry, energy, transport, agriculture and tourism) and assess the manner in which EU policy has defined and implemented sustainability within these fields. It also examines the responses and criticisms of green critics, who argue that the EAPs reflect the continued limitations and weakness of EU action. Finally, it outlines the main provisions of the recent sixth EAP and the initial reaction to the programme, both from the Commission and green NGOs and Members of the European Parliament (MEPs).

The final chapter provides an assessment of the progress that has been made by the EU within the environmental sphere. In doing so, it examines the developments and changes within the EU's attitudes to green politics from three different levels. First, it questions whether or not environmental policy emerging at the EU level has actually made any real impact on the state of the environment. Secondly, it looks at the more indirect impact of an evolving environmental discourse within the EU and asks whether it is possible to identify a changing approach towards green issues at EU level. Thirdly, it looks towards the future for green politics within the EU, identifying potential challenges to further environmental action and assessing the EU's credibility as an environmental actor.

2 |

'Thinking Global, Acting Local': Linking the EU and the Environment

Before attempting to examine the processes and procedures surrounding environmental policy making and politics within the EU, it is important to gain a clearer perspective of what exactly is meant by the term 'environmental politics' and why one might expect the EU to be a major actor within this field. Further, in order to examine and assess the evolution and impact of the EU's actions within the environmental sphere, a frame of reference is required through which this examination can take place.

Changing Attitudes towards the Environment: An Historical Overview

While concern with the natural environment is undoubtedly nothing new, one can identify a distinct change in outlook regarding the political significance of environmental issues from the 1960s onwards. Previously, the environmental focus had rested with issues of wildlife protection and nature conservation. Events in the late 1960s and 1970s, however, sparked a rapid increase in concern for the damage that was being inflicted upon the natural world from the processes of modern industrial society. This concern led to the emergence of new forms of political mobilization, often utilizing unconventional means of protest, leading Robert Nisbit to suggest that:

> When the history of the twentieth century is finally written, the single most important social movement of the period will be judged to be environmentalism (in Dalton 1994: 51).

How can this sudden rise in concern for the environment be explained? Dalton (1994) suggests a convergence of several factors. First, the growth in scientific and educational literature, highlighting the connections between modern industrial processes and environmental destruction. Of particular note, Rachel Carson's (1962) book, *The Silent Spring*, raised public awareness in both America and Europe of the dangers to the environment from the use of man-made chemical fertilizers and pesticides such as DDT. In 1972 the publication of the Club of Rome's *Limits to Growth* report further emphasized the environmental dangers that were facing modern society. The report highlighted what it defined as 'the quantitative restraints of the world environment' and argued for 'the initiation of new forms of thinking that will lead to a fundamental revision of human behaviour' (Meadows *et al.* 1972: 190). For many theorists, the *Limits to Growth* report marks the emergence of the new environmental focus as it implied that there were ecological restraints on the growth of modern society and that technological development may not be enough to combat these problems (see Dobson 1995; Eckersley 1992).

At the same time as this expansion in environmental literature, a number of events also heightened public awareness of environmental dangers. The threat of nuclear war and its potentially destructive effects on the global atmosphere provided a significant spotlight on the potential dangers of scientific and technological development. More directly, a number of environmental disasters vividly highlighted the gap between the growth of modern society and the ability to cope with its consequences. In 1967 the supertanker *Torrey Canyon* discharged millions of gallons of crude oil into the English Channel, causing huge environmental damage to the coastlines of both Cornwall and Brittany. In 1969 a leak of toxins polluted the River Rhine, poisoning the fish and threatening a major source of drinking water for millions of Europeans (Dalton 1993: 51). Such events brought the potential environmental effects of modern industry directly into the homes of the public. The growth in public concern and the emergence of environmental movements was reflected in the first Conference on the Human Environment organized by the United Nations (UN) in Stockholm in 1972.

Despite these signs that national governments were beginning to recognize the dangers of environmental problems, significant action was much slower. The momentum of the environmental movement continued to increase with the emergence of international organizations such as the World Wide Fund for Nature (WWF), Greenpeace and Friends of the Earth (FoE), maintaining media attention and heightening the pressure on governments to act decisively. The arguments of the environmental movement, and a growing body of academic literature were persistently reflected in continued environmental disasters during the late 1970s and 1980s. Further oil spills produced emotive pictures of the vast damage to coastal wildlife, while new scientific research raised concern over the condition of the ozone layer and an emerging process of global warming. The safety of nuclear power also came under the spotlight, first with the accident at Three Mile Island in 1979 and more dramatically with the nuclear disaster at Chernobyl in the Ukraine in 1986. As Dalton suggests, for many the Chernobyl disaster became symbolic of the broader dangers posed by modern industrial society:

> Chernobyl created widespread public recognition that acid rain, dying forests, a decimated ozone layer and nuclear fallout are threats comparable to the economic problems facing advanced industrial societies. Moreover, these environmental problems pose threats that cannot be avoided by individuals because of a privileged social position or geographic location. In short, Chernobyl and its by-products convinced many Europeans that the environmentalists' claims were not mere political rhetoric (Dalton 1993: 58).

This trend has continued throughout the 1980s and 1990s as membership of environmental organizations continues to increase. The movements have not been the only channel for environmental concerns, however. Also during this period European green parties have sought to introduce a green dimension to European party systems, resulting in the election of green members of parliament and more recently green involvement in national government. At the same time, the emergence of a new 'green' consumer culture, most recently personified by the campaigns against genetically modified food, represents another channel of environmental action.

Subsequently, national governments have been forced to tackle the environmental agenda more directly, not only within their own countries but also at international level. Most notable of these events was the UN Conference on Environment and Development in Rio in 1992, which represented one of the largest attempts to confront the underlying causes of international environmental problems. It is within this context of expanding environmental concern and increasing environmental awareness, that one must consider the environmental remit of the EU.

Understanding the Environmental Problem: The Role of Green Political Theory

As with any problem, before seeking solutions, it is first necessary to seek to understand the causes. As identified above, recent decades have witnessed the expansion of an environmental focus and with it has come the emergence of a more coherent ideological approach to understanding our relationship with the natural world. At the heart of the ecological perspective lies a critique of the nature and processes of modern industrial society. The cornerstones of this critique are the claims that modern society must reassess many of its core values and recognize the natural limits which exist to both economic and population growth. As Andrew Dobson summarizes:

> economic growth is prevented not for social reasons—such as restrictive relations of production—but because the Earth itself has a limited carrying capacity (for population), productive capacity (for resources of all types), and absorbent capacity (pollution) (Dobson 1990: 15).

Modern industrial society, it is argued, continues to emphasize growth and expansion as key aspects to a thriving and developing society. In doing so it neglects the limited carrying capacity of the planet, to the detriment of the natural environment.

The inability to recognize and react to this potentially destructive imbalance, it is claimed, is the result of the predominance of 'anthropocentrist' values within modern society. Anthropocentrism places humans as the source of all value, and as such seeks to justify humans' present role of controlling and domineering nature. Zimmerman suggests that this attitude inevitably has significant negative consequences for the natural world, arguing that:

> If humankind is understood as the goal of history, the source of all value, the pinnacle of evolution, and so forth, then it is not difficult for humans to justify the plundering of the natural world, which is not human and therefore 'valueless' (cited in Eckersley 1992: 52).

Within this societal paradigm, nature is valued where and when it has a direct use for modern society. Modern technological developments and the acceptance of the objectivity of natural scientific research, are identified as key dimensions in the continuing process of domination of humans over the rest of the natural world. Further, continuing emphasis upon the values of the 'free market' are seen as instilling within society a strong commitment to the principles of competitiveness and individualism, in which concern for others and for nature have withered. Under these circumstances environmental damage is viewed often as, at best, a secondary concern.

A continuation of this process, it is argued, can only result in severe environmental damage:

> Growth-orientated economies cannot go on using finite resources. Technological innovations cannot solve the problems indefinitely, although appropriate small-scale technologies are seen as one aspect of the solution. Technological advances can only postpone the problems (Vincent 1992: 232).

The ecological critique of modern industrial society represents a reaction against mechanistic science and what are perceived as human attempts to dominate nature through technological development. It claims that if society is to tackle the environmental challenges which it now faces and reverse the process of environmental destruction, it must first seek to develop a different relationship with nature: one where 'humans no longer operate as the "masters" of the natural world but as partners with other living organisms' (Kenny 1994: 218). The focus of green political theory, therefore, rests upon an 'ecocentric' perspective, which seeks to endow all species of life on earth with intrinsic value: a value beyond that which is applied to them by humans. The principle of biospheric equality sees humans as being on an equal level with all other things rather than being their masters. Naess (1973) for example, argues that humans' capacity for freedom depends upon this process of identification with external forces, in particular the natural world. Merchant similarly argues that people must realize that they have a duty to maintain the integrity of the ecosphere (Merchant 1992: 87).[1]

To summarize, therefore, at the heart of interpretations of deep ecology lies the identification of humans as merely one part of the wider ecosphere, dependent upon a balanced relationship with the rest of nature for continued survival. Whereas mainstream Western culture has only seen instrumental value in nature, deep ecology is defined as

1. Deep green philosophy contains a close connection with the concept of holism. This perspective maintains an interconnection between all life on earth. Within such a system, it is impossible to remove or alter one aspect without it having an effect on the overall dynamics of the system itself. The whole, in this case the ecosphere, is seen as greater than the sum of its individual parts. This holistic perspective has a long spiritual tradition running through many cultures.

recognizing the intrinsic value within all species rather than merely identifying nature as a resource for human domination. The implication of developing this more interactive relationship with the natural environment is that this cannot be achieved within a society whose primary aim is economic growth and the short-term pursuit of profit. Hence, the ecological critique argues for a radical overhaul of modern industrial society, including the ideologies and politics upon which it is based.

Different Shades of Green: Alternative Approaches to Environmental Problems

While the identification of environmental problems has produced relative agreement, attitudes towards the practical implementation of solutions have been far more diverse. For many analysts, this diversity is largely dependent upon the issue of 'value' outlined above: in particular how to calculate and assess the value of the natural world and its relationship to modern industrial society. Deep ecology emphasizes that the natural world has a value independent of human assessment. In contrast, however, an alternative form of 'social' ecology has also been identified, which recognizes a more instrumental role for modern society based upon what is defined as a 'light' or 'shallow' green anthropocentrism (see, e.g., Vincent 1992; Eckersley 1992; Kenny 1994). Here, our relationship with nature is identified as one where:

> Humans may play the role of managers of natural processes as long as they act only to enable the natural and diverse evolution of organisms within the biospherical community (Kenny 1994: 240).

From this perspective, the preservation of nature is identified as a key factor for sustaining current standards of living. Hence, rather than just arguing that the natural world should be preserved 'for its own sake' it seeks to demonstrate why this process of preservation is so important for modern industrial society. As Vincent suggests:

> Nature can be an early warning system for us in terms of impending ecological disaster; it supports and nourishes us; we can do valuable experiments on it which can prolong and improve the quality of our lives; we can exercise, admire, relax in ... and be aesthetically moved by its beauty (Vincent 1993: 255).

The identification of nature in terms of 'human value', therefore, enables people to understand the significance that its maintenance holds for human society. This, it is argued, clearly differentiates this ecological approach from anthropocentric perspectives focused upon exploitation of nature for human ends. However, it also remains a significant distance from the ecocentric stance of deep ecology, highlighted earlier.

While these theoretical distinctions may appear largely academic in nature, they play a significant role in the manner in which one can understand the debates and processes which have surrounded attempts to tackle environmental problems over the last 20–30 years. For example, approaches to tackling environmental problems have often been classified as either 'dark' or 'light', or 'deep' or 'shallow' green in nature, depending upon the extent to which they reflect either a radical reshaping of modern industrial society's relationships with the natural world or merely a managerial approach to maintaining valuable natural resources.[2] As will be seen throughout this book, these ideas have an underlying role in our understanding of the conflicts and assessments of both whether the EU represents an effective forum for environmental policy making and whether this policy will actually achieve the environmental objectives identified with it.

Dryzek's (1997) classification of environmental discourses provides a useful example of this broad array of approaches to the environmental question. He suggests a four-fold classification of environmental discourse based around two dimensions (Dryzek 1997: 13). The first dimension reflects either a 'radical' or a 'reformist' relationship to industrialism. The second dimension he identifies as either 'prosaic' or 'imaginative'. Prosaic approaches, he argues, are those whereby the terms of reference reflect those utilized within modern industrial society. Hence, 'the measures endorsed or proposed by these people are essentially those which have been defined by and in industrialism' (Dryzek 1997: 13). Environmental problems therefore can be dealt with within the current frame of reference of industrialism, even though at times this may require a radical alteration in these processes. By contrast, 'imaginative' approaches, Dryzek suggests, require a more fundamental reassessment of the frames of reference within which modern society addresses problems. Within these approaches:

---

2.   For further discussion of these distinctions see Naess 1973, Eckersley 1992, Barry 1994, and also Dobson's (1990) distinction between 'Ecologism' and 'Environmentalism'.

The environment is brought into the heart of society and its cultural, moral, and economic systems, rather than being seen as a source of difficulties standing outside these systems (Dryzek 1997: 13).

These dimensions lead Dryzek to identify the following forms of environmental discourse:

- *Environmental problem solving* (prosaic and reformist) accepts the current political–economic format but seeks to adjust the present system in order to combat emerging environmental problems. These problems are therefore identified as inconvenient 'side-effects' of modern industrial progress. Evident in this form of discourse would be the prioritization of processes such as pricing environmental damage, regulating pollution levels and so on.
- *Survivalism* (prosaic and radical) recognizes that the current processes of economic and population growth will eventually subsume the earth's natural resources and that a radical change is required. However, it still identifies the tools of modern industrialism as the only available methods through which to achieve this change. This discourse is reflected in the 'limits to growth' hypothesis of the Club of Rome, discussed earlier.
- *Sustainability* (imaginative and reformist) attempts to reformulate our understanding and perception of societal growth and development that incorporates the environmental dimension more centrally in the equation. It argues that there is no in-built reason why modern industrial society cannot improve its relationship with nature through this re-evaluation of positive societal development. This was most clearly formulated within the Brundtland Report's (1987) commitment to sustainable development.
- *Green radicalism* (imaginative and radical) rejects the structure and values inherent within modern industrial society and argues for a radical reinterpretation of the human relationship with the rest of the natural world. It claims that modern industrial structures and the continual emphasis upon 'economic growth' and 'development' are incompatible with the radical changes necessary to protect the ecosphere. This discourse reflects many of the concepts outlined within the deep ecology perspective discussed earlier (Dryzek 1997).

It is clearly not enough, therefore, to merely distinguish between those groups who recognize the importance of environmental protection and those who do not. When looking at the evolution of environmental policy making it is also important to examine these processes in the light of the different perceptions of the root cause of the environmental problem and the varying solutions which accompany these perceptions. This provides a clearer understanding of the frames of reference within which to examine the evolution of EU environmental policy making, the influence of different perspectives within this process, and also any significant changes in the underlying perspective of the EU towards environmental problems.

The broad array of approaches and attitudes to environmental issues are reflected in the changing nature of EU environmental policy, both in terms of the policies adopted and the standpoints and debates between the various actors seeking to gain a voice within the policy-making process. As attitudes towards the environment and the significance of this policy dimension have altered within Europe, so one might expect the emphasis upon different forms of environmental discourse to have shifted. A change might also reflect an altered balance between the influence of the different lobby groups active around environmental policy. To gain a clearer picture of the relationship between green politics and the EU, it is clearly important to assess whether the EU's attitude towards environmental problems has evolved to match the development of environmental politics discourse.

The EU as an Environmental Culprit

When initially considering the connections between the EU and the processes of environmental destruction, it is far easier to identify it as a major environmental culprit than as a potential saviour. Indeed, the very rationale behind the emergence of the Union (a group of highly industrialized nations seeking to come together to enhance trade and economic development), would appear to provide the key pressures and conditions, outlined earlier, which have shaped environmental problems over recent decades.

Empirical data enhances this negative perception of the role of Western European countries in the process of environmental destruction. Continued economic growth and increases in both production and consumption, it is argued, are placing severe strains on the natural environment. Hagland, for example, claimed that by the late 1980s acid rain had caused serious damage to historic buildings and 77,000 square miles of European forests. It was also responsible for $1 billion of damage to crops each year in the EU (Hagland 1991: 261). Furthermore, Bomberg states that within the EU countries, emissions of greenhouse gases, such as nitrogen oxide and carbon dioxide, from freight and passenger vehicles rose by 50% between 1973 and 1993 (Bomberg 1998: 12).

EU institutions themselves have acknowledged the 'slow but relentless deterioration' of the European environment (CEC 1992). Commission assessments reflect the continuously increasing pressures placed on natural resources by the member states. These include:

- an estimated 25% increase in car ownership and a 17% increase in mileage between 1990–2000;
- a 63% increase in fertilizer use from 1970–88;
- a 35% increase in solid urban waste from 1987–92;
- a 35% increase in average water use from 1970–85 (CEC 1997: 6).

With these trends in mind, it is unsurprising to find people questioning exactly how the EU can possibly represent a positive force for environmental protection, given its underlying economic rationale and the levels of pollution created by its member states, in order to achieve acceptable levels of economic growth.

A further argument against the European Union concerns a broader green critique of the increasing bureaucratization of modern industrial society and the decreasing levels of individual participation and democracy, as decision making becomes more centralized and removed from local communities.

> The EU represents much that greens instinctively oppose: technocratic policy-making; closed, often murky decision-making procedures; distant institutions, and the dominance of inter-governmental bargaining (Bomberg 1998: 3).

Green politics emphasizes active participation as a key factor in changing attitudes towards the environment. The more people have a say in the decisions that are made, it is argued, the more interest they are likely to have in making an effective change. If people feel that whatever they do will not make a difference, however, and that their voices are not being heard, then it is far harder to gain broad compliance to change. Similarly green politics questions the continued move towards a globalized market, claiming that this ignores key environmental concerns over living within local means and resources, and encourages unsustainable practices.

For many greens, the institutions of the European Union are identified as strong symbols of these processes of centralization and globalization. In particular the status of the Council of Ministers and the alleged 'democratic deficit' are identified as a key cause for concern. The relative weakness of the EP and the large size of members' constituencies are also highlighted within this sphere. Similarly, it is argued that the underlying rationale behind the single European market emphasizes a general pattern of uniformity rather than accommodating and celebrating regional difference.

Despite what would appear a largely negative relationship between developments within the EU and the continuing process of environmental damage, recent years have witnessed a rapid growth in concern for environmental protection at EU level. As Bomberg suggests:

> From an essentially economic community with no firm legal basis for dealing with environmental issues and a clear mandate to facilitate economic growth, the EU has taken on an increasingly central role in policy sectors related to the environment and quality of life (Bomberg 1998: 2).

The EU as an Emerging Environmental Actor

Despite the problems identified above, there are numerous reasons why the EU's emergence as an environmental actor should be viewed as a logical process. These explanations reflect both environmental factors as well as more pragmatic issues concerning economic concerns and the evolution of the EU as a whole.

Given the vastly contrasting nature of the 15 EU member states, identifying a strong rationale for the development of a common environmental policy might initially appear an unlikely proposition. Huge variations exist in terms of population density, urbanization, economic development, geography and climate. In this sense, the EU represents a far from homogeneous region. Indeed this diversity might lead one to argue for national environmental strategies to reflect these differences. In many cases, however, environmental problems are far more international in nature. A recurring theme throughout this book is the claim that environmental problems have little respect for national boundaries; hence environmentally damaging processes in one country can have significant repercussions for others. For example, the impact of the Chernobyl disaster was not contained within the Ukraine, but had devastating effects on vast areas of Europe. Pollution of large rivers, such as that experienced along the Rhine, can equally have a potential impact upon millions of European citizens. Similarly, acid rain which has caused severe damage to lakes and forests in Scandinavia, is the result of industrial processes with a much broader source than just the Nordic countries themselves.

It is clearly not enough, therefore, to provide tight national environmental legislation if you are also at the mercy of the environmental attitudes of other countries. This pattern is clearly reflected within green political thought. For example, Hardin's (1968) ecological analogy of the 'Tragedy of the Commons' highlights the importance of working together in the interests of all, rather than seeking the greatest benefit to the individual. If the environmental balance is to be maintained, he argues, the solutions must lie with collective action. Transposed onto the EU it is obvious that given that member states often share natural resources such as water and air, any environmental problems impacting upon these resources will, by necessity, represent a shared dilemma. Under such circumstances, it is argued, shared problems require shared solutions, which can be most effectively implemented at EU level, while also trying to accommodate the specific national problems and concerns.

Public concern over environmental disasters and ecological threats, such as those outlined earlier, further enhanced the calls for the EU to take action within the environmental sphere. Rapidly expanding support for environmental movements within a number of countries across Europe, most notably Germany, the Netherlands, Belgium and the UK, placed increasing pressure on these national governments to act effectively to curb environmental damage. Further, the election of green party representatives at both national and EU levels demonstrated the political salience of environmental issues. Surveys of public opinion across Europe during the 1980s and 1990s indicated a desire to see environmental protection in Europe organized through the EC/EU because of the inherently cross-border nature of the problems.

One can also expand this rationale beyond the confines of the EU into a broader international and global context. Environmental issues are increasingly being identified as global in nature. As Liefferink *et al.* (1993) points out:

Major problems such as the damage to the ozone layer, the greenhouse effect, the pollution of oceans, the protection of large ecosystems and the conservation of wildlife and habitats, are all predominantly defined in regional or global terms and call for international action (Liefferink *et al.* 1993: 6).

Processes such as the UN conference in Rio increased the drive for international cooperation and negotiation to combat global environmental problems. Within this context, the EU can potentially represent a significant player in these negotiations in a manner in which individual member states cannot.

While most member states were too small individually to play a decisive role in global negotiations, the EU, after 1995, represented 15 countries and 370 million people. A transnational actor of this size was in a powerful position to respond to environmental as well as economic global challenges, or to push others to do so (Bomberg 1998: 35).

The environmental sphere therefore provided an important opportunity for the EU to increase its reputation as a global actor (Bretherton and Vogler 1999). It is undoubtedly in the interests of the EU member states to provide a united front on environmental matters when negotiating their interests on a global scale. Further, commitments made at these negotiations would be far easier to implement uniformly if agreed at EU level rather than purely relying on the will of individual member states.

Explanations for the increasing role of the EU, however, do not only reflect how best to deal with environmental problems. In many cases, the primary motives are much more instrumental than this. In tracing the explanations for the EU's emerging commitment to the environmental policy sphere, it is maybe unsurprising to discover that one can identify at its heart an underlying economic rationale. In particular, there is a strong connection to one of the central principles of the Union: that of equal competition and the development of a common market.

The level of environmental commitment of EU member states varies quite significantly. In effect, there is a three-tier division among member states. At the forefront are the 'leader' states (Austria, Denmark, Finland, Germany, the Netherlands and Sweden), who have faced strong national environmental pressures and have subsequently been active in implementing stricter environmental standards. The 'laggard' states, by contrast, oppose stricter environmental legislation for economic or ideological reasons. These member states (Ireland, Italy, Greece, Portugal and Spain) argue that the cost of implementing stricter environmental standards and the pressures which this would place upon their competitiveness make such standards a relatively low priority. In Spain, for example, priority has been given to improving living standards and to generating employment, both of which, they argue, could be hindered by the imposition of the environmental standards of the 'rich north' (Sbragia 1996: 249). Importantly, the environment in these four countries is not as politically salient an issue as it is in many northern states and as a result there is not the same domestic pressure from environmental groups and parties (Butt Philip 1998: 262). Between these two positions, one can identify the remaining 'ambivalent' member states (Belgium, France, Luxembourg and the UK). While these states are certainly more committed to environmental protection than the 'laggard' states, they tend to support specific environmental measures rather than adopting the more consistently 'green' line of the 'leader' states.

This division among member states' attitudes towards environmental issues created significant problems for the EU. While 'leader' countries sought to introduce quite stringent environmental measures, often as a result of strong public pressure and the electoral salience of green issues in these countries, other EU member states, especially the 'laggard' states, developed little or no environmental regulation of their own. This discrepancy between EU member states meant that industry within those countries which had introduced strict environmental regulations would potentially be at a competitive disadvantage to their rivals in other countries, where environmental costs were not part of the production equation. Given this imbalance there was clearly an economic rationale for those states actively initiating and implementing increasing levels of environmental legislation to find a method of removing this competitive disadvantage.

For the leader states, therefore, the introduction of environmental policies at EU level reflected a desire to prevent 'distortion of competition' in the single market, as high environmental standards would clearly put them at a competitive disadvantage. It was in the economic interests of these countries to 'spread the higher costs of compliance by means of stricter environmental laws across the whole EU' (Butt Philip 1998: 262). Consequently, the leader states tend to act as policy initiators seeking to raise EU environmental standards to their own national standards. This has often resulted in the implementation of EU standards which go beyond the lowest standards necessary to correct negative externalities (Hix 1999: 224-26).

Support for a more unified EU approach to environmental regulation also came from among multi-national firms who had operations spanning many of the EU member states. While these firms were not necessarily supportive of stricter environmental controls, they did recognize the value of developing common environmental standards throughout the EU. It was suggested that if they did have to deal with environmental regulations, it would be operationally easier to have one set of rules to comply with rather than a different set of rules and regulations for each country (Connelly and Smith 1999: 262).

The EU's central commitment to comparable standards between member states to ensure equal competition provided strong justification for the evolution of environmental standards across EU member states. This was despite the fact that the environment had not been part of the original objectives of the Treaty of Rome. This economic rationale would appear to be one of the primary factors in explaining the rapid expansion of EU activity within the environmental sphere. As Connelly and Smith summise:

> legislation in these [environmental] matters was necessary, not directly for environmental protection *per se*, but to secure protection of the primary purpose of the community, that is, the achievement of an economic common market. Environmental concern was thus contingent on the primary rationale of the Community (Connelly and Smith 1999: 226).

That environmental policy issues have developed into a significant aspect of EU activity also reflects a commitment from within the European Commission to push forward this policy sphere. Again, however, there is a more complex explanation for this commitment than merely an altruistic concern for the environment. As Chapter 3 explains, environmental policy provided an area in which the Commission could advance EU policy during a period of relative Eurosclerosis in the 1970s.

Environmental policy, therefore, originally represented a policy sphere where the initiatives of the Commission were not constantly competing with entrenched concerns of member states to maintain their national interests. While many member states had little or no substantial environmental policy, those countries that had adopted environmental policies, as mentioned above, were keen to see them expanded throughout Europe. Additionally, public support for environmental action made national governments reluctant to strangle policy initiatives. Eurobarometer surveys during this period highlighted a significant level of support from among EU citizens for a common European policy for protecting the environment (Bomberg 1998: 13). Given these conditions there was clear justification for the Commission to take an active lead in this sphere. Member states rarely questioned the legitimacy of its activities regarding environmental policy, allowing a relatively rapid manoeuvre in the environmental field. Given this relative freedom to develop policy, therefore, the EU has swiftly expanded its environmental dimension to the point where, as Freestone suggests, it has become:

> one of the more successful policies of the Community, both in terms of
> the areas of activity that it commands and the degree of popular support
> which it is beginning to command (Freestone 1991: 135).

To summarize, a broad set of factors have contributed to the emergence of the EU as a key player within environmental policy and politics. While it is fair to acknowledge that environmental explanations clearly exist as to why the EU *should* be seeking to take a lead, it has more often been alternative pressures which have been at the forefront of actually accounting for why the EU *has* tackled environmental problems. Within the latter it is evident that the EU's environmental 'enthusiasm' appears closely linked to the broader context of the processes of Union evolution and development; in particular the development of the single market.

Green Politics and the EU: Assessing the Connections

This chapter has sought to identify the connections between the emergent issues and themes within green politics and the development of the EU's commitment to environmental protection. While it is clear that one cannot identify the impetus for this environmental commitment purely from an altruistic concern for green issues, what is evident is that the increased public interest and commitment to green political issues more generally, has been mirrored in the development of EU policy-making within this sphere. As Bomberg suggests:

> The 'greening' of European politics and the acceleration of European
> integration have become intertwined: European integration has been a
> boon to green activism, whilst the EU's institutional development has

been spurred by the rise of green concerns on Europe's political agenda (Bomberg 1998: 2).

While the adoption of an environmental commitment represents a significant development within EU policy making, the exact nature and extent of the 'green' dimension within the EU is still open to debate. The EU has much to do even to convince environmentalists that it can be an effective environmental actor, rather than an environmental culprit. Questions also remain over the underlying commitment of the EU to environmental issues. The drive towards developing an environmental dimension has not always rested solely with a commitment to green issues and ideas, but has also reflected other overriding motives regarding both equal competition and maintaining the momentum of EU policy development.

In addition, even if the EU does seek to tackle environmental problems, questions still remain over exactly what approaches it should adopt in tackling these issues. Hence, when looking at the emergence of policy and increasing pressure around environmental concerns it is important to consider the different perspectives of the actors involved. Dryzek's (1997) categorization may provide a useful guide in this respect. While the EU may seek to improve environmental conditions, the environment remains only one small aspect of its activities and interests. As such, it must shape its commitment to green issues within the overall parameters of its broader aims and objectives. While green voices provide one set of solutions they are not necessarily the most popular. As would be expected, other interested groups are keen to provide an alternative perspective on environmental issues and EU priorities. This book identifies an emerging environmental dimension shaped by a broad array of different pressures and perspectives.

The remainder of this book will help to demonstrate how the green dimension within the EU has been shaped by alternative perceptions of environmental problems, such as those outlined earlier in this chapter, and the potential solutions that accompany them. To what extent has a green political philosophy been able to infiltrate and influence the processes of policy development within the EU, or do the environmental policies which have emerged merely pay lip service to the central aims of green politics?

3 |

Developing a Green Agenda: The Emergence of Environmental Policy within the European Union

The Environmental Policy of the then European Economic Community (EEC) between 1957 and 1972 has been described as a series of 'incidental' measures (Hildebrand 1993: 17). There was no explicit mention of the environment in the Treaty of Rome 1957, although this is not surprising given public opinion at the time. For example, even the constitution of the Netherlands, which is viewed as a 'green' state, did not contain any reference to the environment until 1982 (Liefferink 1997: 218). The focus of the EEC then was primarily to establish a common market and to ensure economic growth. Despite this, expansion of policy competence did occur in the environmental field, mainly through a broad interpretation of the EEC Treaty, especially Article 2, which called on the Community to promote a 'harmonious development of economic activities, a continuous and balanced expansion, an increase in stability, an accelerated raising of the standard of living and closer relations between the states belonging to it'. Interpreting 'standard of living' to include environmental protection allowed environmental legislation to be 'smuggled' into Community law.

As the environment was not one of the common policies listed in Article 3, the main legal bases for action were Articles 94 and 308. Both provided a tentative constitutional foundation for the EC's actions in this area. Article 94 allows for the Council to 'issue directives for the approximation of such provisions laid down by law, regulation or administrative action in Member States as directly affect the establishment or functioning of the common market'. Article 308 additionally allows the Council, acting unanimously on a proposal from the Commission, to take appropriate measures 'necessary to attain, in the course of the operation of the common market, one of the objectives of the

Community' where there is no treaty provision, although this was seen as a last resort. An excellent example of the type of policy adopted during this period was the 1967 Directive harmonizing the classification, packaging and labelling of dangerous substances, something that was clearly related to the functioning of the common market, but also had an environmental impact. An important aspect of both articles is the fact that both need unanimity in the Council, with the EP only having the right to be consulted.

The emergence of environmental policy was based solely on a broad interpretation of the Treaty of Rome, which allowed the Community to pass a number of initial pieces of environmental legislation, although the need for unanimity and the restricted basis for action under Article 94 circumscribed the development of EEC environmental policy. It is clear that the environmental legislation passed in this period—nine directives and one regulation—'cannot be regarded as adding up to any sort of proper and coherent policy' (Hildebrand 1993: 19). This is hardly surprising given the political climate of the time, with the green movement largely in its infancy and environment problems not seen as salient political issues.

1972–86

The 1972 Stockholm UN Conference on the Human Environment can be identified as a major turning point in the development of EC environment policy. Growing public concern about environmental problems and rising support for green parties and pressure groups put the issue high on the international political agenda. Although the UN meeting was influential in focusing the minds of the EU leaders, so was the introduction of German environmental legislation, as it meant that environmental legislation was needed to eliminate trade distortions between member states (Bretherton and Vogler 1999: 81). The response to both developments was an EU Heads of State Summit in Paris, 1972, where the leaders declared that:

> economic expansion is not an end in itself ... it should result in an improvement in the quality of life as well as in the standard of living ... particular attention will be given to intangible values and to protecting the environment so that progress may really be put at the service of mankind (in Liefferink *et al.* 1993: 3).

As Jordan notes, today this seems like a statement of the obvious, but at the time 'it marked a sea change in political opinion' (Jordan 1999a: 3). The leaders invited the Community institutions to develop an action programme on the environment, which resulted in the first EAP being launched, in 1973.

The most important developments came towards the end of this period. The European Court of Justice (ECJ), in a landmark case (C-91 and 92/79), offered support to the Commission by upholding the use of Article 94 as a base for environmental policy. It held that environmental provisions could be based on this article provided they were linked to the setting up or operation of the internal market. The ECJ also ruled that environmental protection justified certain limitations on the free movement of goods. In a 1985 judgment relating to the implementation of the Waste-Oils Directive, it ruled that:

> The principle of freedom of trade is not to be viewed in absolute terms but is subject to certain limits justified by the objectives of general interest pursued by the Community ... The Directive must be seen in the perspective of environmental protection, which is one of the Community's essential objectives (in Jordan 1999a: 8-9).

As there was no inclusion of the environment into the Treaties, this was a reinterpretation of the basic mission of the EC based upon the informal integration within this field since the Treaty of Rome in 1957. As can be seen, the interest in environmental policy was spurred

> not so much by an upsurge of post-industrialist values and the Nine's endeavours to create a 'Human Union' or to give the EC a 'human face' as by the realisation that widely differing national rules on industrial pollution could distort competition: 'dirty states' could profit economically (Lodge 1989: 320).

In short, 'community environmental policy was incidental to measures to harmonise laws in order to abolish obstacles to trade between member states' (in Judge 1993: 3).

The result of this informal integration was a significant increase in EU environmental legislation. Between 1973 and 1985 120 directives, 27 decisions and 14 regulations were implemented, meaning that proposals on the environment constituted the fastest growing area of EU policy. It is, however, important to consider the context of this huge increase in environmental legislation that can, in part, be explained by the fact that the EEC was starting from such a low base prior to 1973. Haigh argued that, despite the quantitative rise, this period represented the 'dark ages' of EU environmental policy. He suggests that the use of unanimity and lowest common denominator bargaining in the Council had a detrimental effect upon policy decisions (in Jordan 1999a: 7). As this period can be seen to coincide with the general 'Eurosclerosis' that affected the Union after the resurgence of intergovernmentalism and the aftermath of the 1973 oil price rises, this would be unsurprising. If the whole European project was seen to be stagnating, why should environmental legislation be any different? Haigh's view has been criticized by Majone, who argues that

> the rate of growth of environmental legislation appears to have been largely unaffected by the political vicissitudes, budgetary crises, and the recurrent waves of Europessimism of the 1970s and early 1980s (Majone 1994: 85).

In light of this, the rise in environmental legislation, even if its quality is debatable, represents a major achievement.

Single European Act: 1987–92

As highlighted, EC environmental policy had so far developed in the absence of an evolution of its formal legal basis, evolving through almost total reliance upon Articles 94 and 308. With the advent of the SEA, this changed. Amendments to the EC Treaty saw the introduction of a whole title (Title VII) dedicated to the environment. It appeared in Part Three, 'Policy of the Community'. With this, the EU finally gained explicit competence to act in the environment field. Articles 174-76 (130r-t) provided this, although to a large extent the areas of activity were not new, as the SEA essentially gave the EC competence where it was already active.

Article 174 (130r) listed the principles of Community environmental 'action', which is explored in more detail below. Article 175 (130s) identified the legislative procedures to be adopted, which mainly involved unanimity in the Council, with a consultative role for the EP. Finally, Article 176 (130t) allowed member states to maintain or intro-duce more stringent protective measures as long as they were compat-ible with the rest of the Treaty. Article 94, which had assisted the EC in developing a body of environmental legislation, was now accompanied by Article 95 (100a) which instructed the Commission to take 'as a base a high level of [environmental] protection' when proposing measures for the establishment and functioning of the internal market.

The new article also facilitated decision making in that proposals were to be adopted by the Council acting by qualified majority voting (QMV). The EP's powers were increased too, proposals under Article 95 being subject to the cooperation procedure. Finally, a derogation clause was inserted (previously Article 100a[4]), which allowed member states, after a harmonizing measure had been adopted, to apply national provisions *inter alia*, to protect the environment.

The SEA therefore created a confusing legislative structure for the environment, with a distinction being drawn between environmental legislation linked to the completion of the single market on the one hand, and legislation designed to protect the environment on the other. This in itself would be problematic, but the fact that different legislative procedures applied in each case adds to this confusion. It also created a situation whereby the Commission and NGOs attempted to create links between the legislation and the single market to ensure that it went through under the more favourable Article 95 rather than Article 175. This left the Commission open to legal challenges as the use of the wrong legal basis for legislation could be challenged before the ECJ as an abuse of the principles of institutional balance. On a more positive note, the SEA in Articles 95 and 176 recognized the right of member states to maintain higher standards in this field.

The recurring tension between high environmental standards and maintenance of the single market is evident within the SEA. Deciding which environmental measures are linked to trade harmonization and which are not, can be a matter of interpretation. Resolving this conflict has often been left to the ECJ, which has been shown to favour maximalist interpretations of European law in many cases. An excellent example of this tension, and the influence of the ECJ, was the Danish bottle case. In the 1980s Denmark passed legislation to the effect that all beer bottles sold in Denmark had to be recyclable. This legislation meant that Denmark had higher standards than the rest of the EU. Non-Danish brewers argued that this law constituted a restraint of trade as distance made it difficult for them to retrieve and re-use the beer bottles, a problem not faced by Danish brewers. The case went to the ECJ which ruled in 1988, clearly mindful of the recent introduction of Article 174 into the SEA, that while the law did restrain trade, it had legitimate environmental protection aims and would be allowed to stand. As Weale argues, 'the ECJ has therefore both supported strong environmental measures and made their passage easier' (Weale 1996: 597).

While the SEA failed to resolve the tension between trade and environmental protection and began the ambiguity over the use of Articles 95 and 175, it can be seen as a 'watershed' in the development of the EU's environmental policy. Many argued, based upon an interpretation of the SEA's amendments, that for the first time it was, *de jure*, correct to speak of an EU environmental policy (Bomberg 1998: 36-37; Hildebrand 1993: 33).

The Treaty on European Union to Amsterdam, 1993–98

EU environmental policy was strengthened and extended by the Treaty on European Union (TEU) in 1993. It built upon the SEA provisions, but also tried to clarify some of the ambiguity in the Treaty.

According to Church and Phinnemore (1994: 232), the main difference between the treatment of the environment in the SEA and the TEU was a qualitative one. Article 174 stated that the EC was only competent to pursue 'action' relating to the environment, whereas post-TEU, the reference is to 'Community policy on the environment'. It also received a heightened profile, with 'environment protection' being mentioned in the Preamble to the TEU, with respect for the environment being inserted into the principles of the EC (Article 2), and 'a policy in the sphere of the environment' being explicitly listed in Article 3 as an activity of the EC. The TEU also set out to simplify EU decision making in general, and especially to try and clarify the confusion caused by Articles 95 and 175.

To a large extent, the long-standing tension between trade and environment remained unresolved, with the conflict of the legal basis of action between the 'environment procedure' (Article 175) and the 'approximation of laws' procedure for the internal market (Article 95) allowing member states to decide how strictly to interpret and implement the rules. This conflict related to the degree to which member states are able to impose stricter standards than those agreed at the Community level. The compromises on decision-making procedures meant that they remained complex, with four procedures now applicable to different types or aspects of 'environmental' legislation. Article 95 remained largely unchanged, although the EP was given the right of co-decision, increasing the powers of the EP, an institution traditionally sympathetic to green concerns, vis-à-vis the Council in this aspect of environmental policy.

The general application of QMV to Article 175 was blocked by the Spanish government, resulting in three different voting procedures. The general application was QMV in the Council and cooperation with the EP, although for 'general action programmes', which set out the priority objectives to be attained, the EP gained the right of co-decision. For measures involving taxation, town and country planning, land use and choice of energy, however, unanimity remained in the Council and the EP was only to be consulted. Instead of clarifying the legislative procedures, the TEU actually presented policy makers with a legal minefield (Butt Philip 1998: 260).

The Treaties of Amsterdam and Nice: 1999–2001

On 1 May 1999 the Treaty of Amsterdam came into force after ratification by the last member state, France, initiating the fifth phase of the historical development of European environmental policy. Environment was one of the few policy areas to be comprehensively reviewed at the 1996–97 Intergovernmental Conference (IGC). This revision was designed to try and rectify some of the criticisms of the TEU's provisions on the environment, which to a large extent reflect Vogel's view that when the Community is faced with a tension between environmental protection and economic integration, 'it chooses the latter over the former' (Vogel 1993: 127).

The impact of the Amsterdam Treaty concerned tasks, principles and decision making. On the former, 'respect for the environment' in Article 2 of the Treaty of Rome was reinforced. Henceforth, the Community was to promote 'a high level of protection and improvement of the quality of the environment'. The EU's ability to do this was enhanced by the insertion of a new Article 6, which declared that 'environmental protection requirements must be integrated into the definition and implementation of the Community policies and activities … in particular with a view to promoting sustainable development'. With regard to decision making, one development was to include the Committee of the Regions for consultation under Article 175. Secondly, Amsterdam managed to simplify the decision-making procedures, by reducing them mainly to co-decision and simple consultation. Co-decision applies for general environmental measures, Article 175(1) and with the environmental action programmes, Article 175 (3). Therefore both now follow the standard community model. Here the right of initiative lies with the

Commission, the Council and EP co-decide, and QMV is used in the Council. Decision making is different under Article 175(2), which deals with taxes, town and country planning, land use or energy supply. Here the Commission still has the right of initiative, but the Council voting rule is unanimity and the EP is only consulted. This simplification is intended to make environmental policy clearer and also to reduce the risk of conflict on the legal base for a measure noted earlier. Article 95 was amended to clarify the provisions when countries can adopt higher environmental standards. Governments can now, once a Community measure had been adopted, keep existing national provisions or introduce higher environmental standards than those set for the EU as a whole, as long as they were based upon scientific evidence. This proviso was inserted at the behest of the Mediterranean states who were worried that this 'legislation-up' could lead to stricter Community legislation in the future (Barnes and Barnes, 1999: 18-19).

The Treaty of Nice (December 2000) altered very little of the environmental *acquis communautaire*. This is perhaps unsurprising, as Collier notes, the important principles are already in existence and the real issue at stake is whether there is sufficient political will to push ahead with implementing existing legislation in a way that benefits environmental protection (Collier 1997: 19). The main development was that Article 175(2) was broadened to ensure that '*measures significantly affecting quantitative* management of water resources or *interfering with the availability of those resources*' required unanimity (amendments in italics). This was inserted at the behest of the Portuguese, who obtain the majority of their water from rivers that originate in Spain. The rest of the Article remained the same, which means that taxation matters still require unanimity. This was a significant disappointment to many green parties and NGOs, who felt that their increased participation in government might see QMV extended to matters of environmental taxation, which could in turn lead to a change of heart towards EU-wide eco-taxes.

The Principles and Objectives of EU Environmental Policy

Having seen how provisions for EC environmental policy have developed through the Treaties since 1957, this section identifies the major principles and objectives of this policy since it became a Community competence in 1987. The principles of EU environmental policy could also be found in the first EAP, which is considered in more detail in Chapter 5. Here the discussion will be confined to only those principles that have been formally incorporated into the Treaties.

The SEA established a clear set of objectives for environmental policy. It introduced Article 174 (130r), which spelt out the objectives that underlie the EU's environmental policy. They are:

- to preserve, protect and improve the quality of the environment;
- to contribute towards protecting human health;
- to ensure a prudent and rational utilization of natural resources.

As can be seen, these are broad objectives, which could bring nearly all environmental issues within the competence of Community legislation (Hildebrand 1993: 34). It is more important to consider the principles of EU environmental policy as established by the SEA, as they provide a more accurate picture of what EU policy in this area could achieve. The principles include:

- the preventative principle;
- the polluter-pays principle;
- rectification of environmental pollution at source when possible;
- the principle that environmental protection requirements must be integrated into the definition and implementation of other Community policies.

The preventative principle starts from the assumption that 'prevention is better than cure'. The 'prevention principle' is important as it tries to tackle pollution at source and is based upon a belief in the ability of technological solutions to these problems (Connelly and Smith 1999: 228-29). It therefore encourages people and organizations to be pro-active in relation to the environment rather than just reactive. It also reflects environmentalist claims to rebalance the pressure of argument away from those seeking to save the environment to those wishing to pollute, by making them justify why they must pollute. The adoption of this principle by the SEA was seen as an important change of policy by the EU.

'Polluter-pays' attempts to incorporate the externalities into production costs, ensuring the final costs are more accurate (Connelly and Smith 1999: 163-65). Raising the cost aims to encourage polluters to find less polluting products and technologies. Both principles are integral parts of the economic problem-solving dialogue and form the basis of much EU thinking.

Rectification of environmental damage at source means that preference is given to emission limits over quality standards. The integration principle recognizes that environmental problems are cross-sectional and cannot be tackled without other common policies taking account of their impact upon the environment. Two excellent examples to illustrate this point are the Common Agricultural Policy (CAP) and the Structural Funds. Both have the capability to negate any positive environmental impact of the EU environmental policy as a whole. Indeed Article 174 makes this explicit by stating that 'environmental protection must be a component of the EU's other policies'. This was the beginning of a process culminating in the fifth EAP and the attempts to fully integrate the environment into all EU policy areas. It does not mean, however, that environmental protection should always prevail in clashes with other policy areas. Rather it suggests that if an objective can be achieved in a variety of ways the environmentally least harmful approach should be adopted. The SEA also established clearer guidelines for developing new policies, based on:

- available scientific and technical data;
- the environmental conditions in the various parts of Europe;
- the likely costs and benefits of acting and of not acting;
- the economic and social development of the Community as a whole and the balanced development of its regions;
- action at the most appropriate level (subsidiarity).

Why did the SEA lead to stricter EU environmental regulation? Apart from trying to ensure a level-playing field, the SEA was an attempt to address the market failures inherent in the single market. Environmental pollution can be seen as an unwanted side effect of human economic activity. When this impact is not included in the market price of goods, it is termed an 'externality'. Therefore, the fact that the costs of environmental pollution are not included in the price of goods can be seen as a 'negative externality' (Connelly and Smith 1999: 132). A number of policy options are available to limit these market failures and as a result of the SEA, the EU has attempted to regulate environmental standards at all stages of the economic process: production (chemical emissions), distribution (eco-labelling), consumption (vehicle emissions), and disposal (waste management). Clearly, without environmental standards and environmental labelling, both business and consumers cannot possess the information they need to make judgments about the environmental quality of the goods they buy and sell, with implications for trade within the internal market.

To the principles contained in the SEA, the TEU added the 'precautionary principle' and the commitment that the EU should aim for a high level of environmental protection. The inclusion into Article 174 of the 'precautionary principle', based upon the German *Vorsorgeprinzip*, was aimed at strengthening the preventative principle of the SEA (Bomberg 1998: 38). While appearing similar, the precautionary principle suggests that action should be taken even before a definite causal link has been established between an activity and any consequent harm to the environment. Although the EU has not defined this principle, it can be argued that its meaning can be interpreted from international agreements signed by the EU (Connelly and Smith 1999: 230). Importantly, it has been suggested that the inclusion of this principle has altered the nature of debate from 'disputes on *whether* action should be taken' towards a greater emphasis upon '*which* measures should be taken and *when*' (in Bomberg 1998: 38, emphasis added).

Sustainable Development

The EU was granted 'full participant status' at the 1992 Rio Earth Summit, giving it many of the same rights as the participating states (Bretherton and Vogler 1999: 91). Despite this, the Treaty revision that occurred in the same year at Maastricht did not explicitly incorporate the commitment made to sustainable development at Rio. The TEU did give a legal base for the concept of sustainable development, based upon the Brundtland Report's definition, which states that the EU should aim for development that 'meets the needs of the present without compromising the ability of future generations to meet their own needs' (1987: 8). Although the term is used in the TEU, it is not used consistently. For example, Baker highlights the 'confusing situation whereby the Maastricht Treaty speaks of "sustainable progress", "sustainable growth" and "sustainable development"' (Baker 1997: 92). The clearest illustration of the weak commitment can be found in the TEU revised Article 2 which calls for 'sustainable and non-inflationary growth respecting the environment'. Clearly, the most important focus here is on non-inflationary growth. This situation was compounded by the fact that the fifth EAP refers explicitly to 'sustainable development' throughout. The action programme and Treaties appeared to be pursuing different goals.

In part, this reflects the different actors responsible for producing the documents. The fifth EAP reflected mainly the thinking of Directorate General (DG) Environment (formerly DGXI), while the Treaties reflect the general climate of opinion among government leaders at the time. Why is this inconsistency so significant? First, Baker argues that the ambivalence in the wording may produce inconsistency in the development of EU environmental policy. Secondly, she argues that it may suggest the EU is reverting back to its 'old strategy of economic development based on growth onto which environmental considerations can be grafted' (Baker 1997: 93). Finally, any moves away from sustainable development to sustainable growth could have a major impact upon policy development. This is because the former is a much broader concept that includes quality objectives, such as quality of life, the right to participation, and social justice, while the latter merely focuses on quantity (Collier 1997: 4).

To some extent the Amsterdam Treaty tackled many of these problems. Although it did not go as far as some member states wished in the field of environmental protection, it did contain a less equivocal commitment to sustainable development. The principle was included in the Preamble and in the objectives of the EU, as well as Article 2, which lays down the tasks of the EU. Article 2 now calls for 'a harmonious, balanced and sustainable development of economic activities'. Jordan highlights the fact that sustainable development should be the guiding objective of all the EU's policies across all three pillars, which raises the possibility of environmental concerns moving away from just Pillar One (Jordan 1999a: 12). The Treaty also reflects a concern to ensure intersectoral coordination in Article 6, which states that

> environmental protection requirements must be integrated into the
> definition and implementation of Community policies and activities ...
> in particular with a view to promoting sustainable development.

Critics point to the fact that the Treaty still refers to both sustainable development and growth and argue that this is formal recognition that the EU remains committed only to a version of weak sustainability, based upon an anthropocentric view of the world, which calls for environmental protection 'for the sake of human welfare, rather than for the sake of ecosystems preservation *per se*' (Collier 1997: 4).

Decision-making Rules

In the development of EU environmental action, both in legal and policy terms, what is clear is that the motor of integration has been the Commission (Butt Philip 1998: 261). The big questions that need to be addressed here, using the framework outlined in Chapter 1, are how the Commission was able to develop an *acquis* on the environment without a legal basis and without member states raising serious objections.

History-making and National Diversity
'History-making' decisions are those decisions that change the nature of the EU. They alter procedures, rebalance the powers of the institutions and expand the policy remit of EU. These history-making decisions set the overall policy framework for the EU, but they tend to have little impact on the day-to-day policy decisions taken by the EU. In order to identify how the history-making decisions that shaped the development of EU environmental policy were made, it is crucial to understand the different national interests and styles. Given the contrasting attitudes identified in Chapter 2 it is fair to question why EU member states have ever agreed to policy measures that went 'beyond any conceivable standards that would be strictly necessitated by a concern to ensure a single functioning market' (Weale 1996: 598).

In the early days of environmental policy, many argued that the member states were either unconcerned or too preoccupied to worry about the development of this new policy area. Jordan argues that the states appeared content during the 1970s to let the policy develop under its own impetus with little supervision of the Commission (Jordan 1999a: 4). The Commission was able to use the Monnet method to coax member states into deeper integration than they may have wished to see. This was supported by the ECJ rulings on the use of Article 95 and 308, that tended to favour a maximalist approach to integration. The member states were also preoccupied with the aftermath of the 'empty chair' crisis and squabbles over creating the internal market. Therefore, the Commission which found its room for manoeuvre in many policy areas blocked by the member states, found that 'it was pushing at an open door in developing an environmental agenda for the EC in the 1970s' (Butt Philip 1998: 261). Even the laggard states with little or no environmental policy of their own realized that environmental issues 'know no borders'.

The importance of the environmental issue in many leader countries means that, in order to get higher standards, these countries are willing to compromise with the laggards. For example, the main environmental Title in the SEA was a result of a bargain between the leaders and laggards. Environmental standards were introduced at the cost of more aid, in this case Structural Funds, to help the laggards meet these new standards. A similar bargain in 1992 'bought' Spanish support for the extension of QMV with an increase in cohesion funds. This resulted in Spain receiving 7.9 billion ECU between 1993–99, one-third of which was specifically intended for environmental improvements (Morata and Font 1998: 222). Policy compromise can also be achieved through 'burden sharing' or flexible targets. Poorer member states are often given less stringent targets or more time to achieve them, especially when the EU tries to present a common position in global negotiations. This compromise is, unsurprisingly, controversial as different states have different burdens. The dilemma faced by some member states is vividly summed up thus: 'we don't want to let other Member States do bugger all while we spend billions to meet standards' (Peterson and Bomberg 1999: 184-85).

These compromise debates revolve around the principle of subsidiarity, which is intended to ensure that decisions are taken at the most appropriate level. Interestingly, the first mention of the concept can be found in the SEA under Article 174, so for seven years it only applied to environmental policy (Connelly and Smith 1999: 233). In the TEU, the principle was extended to all of the EU's activities. Article 5 (3b) sets out the basic principles underlying subsidiarity and establishing when the EU has competence to act:

> In areas which do not fall within its exclusive competence, the Community shall take action ... only if and in so far as the objectives of the proposed action cannot be sufficiently achieved by the member states and therefore, by reason of scale or effects of the proposed action, be better achieved by the Community.

The basic premise is that the EU can only act in matters at which it is the most appropriate level for action. What the most appropriate level is remains unclear, as there was dispute over the political and legal meaning of the principle. This ambiguity allowed all member states to support the principle. A number of 'leader' countries saw it as a way of preserving their stronger regulatory traditions and also increasing EU involvement because, as pollution knows no borders, the EU is inevitably the best level to deal with environmental issues. 'Laggard' states saw it as a way of challenging whether the EU level was the most appropriate for action and those who fear further EU involvement in domestic politics can claim that this holds back further encroachment. At the time, there was a view that subsidiarity might mean the repeal of EU legislation and the 'renationalization' of policy, although in practice the main development was the Commission watering down controversial legislative proposals (Collier and Golub 1997: 239). This highlights the ongoing conflict between whether the national or supranational level was the most appropriate for environmental policy. Despite these negatives, subsidiarity can also be identified as conforming to the desire of many green parties and NGOs to see decisions made as close to the people as possible.

The final argument relates to one of economic necessity. In an increasingly global marketplace it is argued that the country with the highest environmental standards will become the benchmark for others to follow. Therefore, the EU must legislate for high environmental standards on a par with those found in North American and Japanese markets in order to take advantage of possible economies of scale (Weale 1996: 601). This is linked to the argument over a California or Delaware effect (Hix 1999: 226). In Delaware, regulatory competition was seen to have a deregulatory effect, as the state used an absence of regulation to attract investment. Yet regulation upwards can also attract investment, with California being identified as a good example of an environmental leader both in the USA and internationally.

At the EU level, many states may wish to see higher environmental standards for the reasons outlined, but due to the issue's lack of salience or coalition difficulties nationally, they may be unable to push forward the domestic legislation necessary. EU environmental legislation may be seen as another case of member states using the EU to force through unpopular decisions that national politicians are unwilling or unable to adopt at home. Thus,

> at home, ministers denounce and disown the policies for which they themselves have voted in Brussels. They conceal and deny transfers of sovereignty enshrined in treaties that they have helped to draft ... They do all this because there is no easier way to fudge responsibility for an unpopular decision than to blame it on 'Brussels' (*The Economist* 23 October 1999: 8).

The laggard countries, having accepted the need for environmental protection, may be willing to accept EU legislation as a necessary evil. For example, Spain adopted the whole corpus of EU legislation after entry to the EU in 1986 with little attention paid to the economic implications (Weale 1996: 599). With enlargement high on the EU's political agenda, it is worth noting here the views of the accession states, especially the Visegrad 4 (Czech Republic, Hungary, Poland, and Slovakia). The environment was virtually ignored under state socialism and the transition to a capitalist market economy has done little to improve the major environmental problems these countries face. A condition of joining the club is that new members adopt the rules of the EU (the *acquis communautaire*) in full, including all environmental legislation. The need to fully implement the *acquis* is important for two reasons. First, it prevents possible distortions of trade within the newly expanded single market, highlighting once again the connection between the environment and trade within the EU. Secondly, environmental degradation in the East has a negative impact on Western Europe. This was graphically demonstrated in February 2000 when a cyanide leak from a Romanian gold mine polluted the Tisza in Hungary and the Danube in Yugoslavia. High environmental standards in the West are potentially rendered meaningless if the new member states do not have similar standards, but meeting the commitments of the *acquis* will undoubtedly impose major costs on the accession states. To counter this, a number of assistance programmes have been set up and environmental assistance also forms a major part of Agenda 2000 (Francis 1999: 169). The main problem is that, like many of the other 'laggard' states, the environment is not as politically salient as other issues, especially those related to economic development. It is therefore likely that, whereas the last enlargement to include Austria, Finland, and Sweden increased the number of leader states, this enlargement is likely to shift the balance back in favour of the laggards, 'making the EU (even) more diverse than it is now' (Liefferink and Andersen 1998: 255).

Setting Policy: The Systemic Level and the Institutions
An understanding of history-making decisions is crucial to explain why the EC obtained competence in environmental policy and also to explain the general direction which that policy takes. These types of decisions tend to focus on the process of European integration, so to

understand what Hix calls, the *politics* of the EU, or what Peterson calls *day-to-day* decisions (in Cram 1996: 54), it is important to examine how policy is 'set' by institutions and how the policy is 'shaped' by actors within the institutions and other interest groups.

'Policy-setting' occurs at the end of the EU's legislative process. Policies can be said to have been 'set' when directives or other legislative tools are issued. This type of decision making tends to follow the standard community method of 'Commission proposes, Council disposes, EP amends'. The result is that agreements need to be secured

> both within and between key institutional actors (the Commission, the Council, the Parliament and the Court), as well as with the functional constituencies of important interest groups. The result is a 'joint-decision trap' ... in which the status quo is given privileged place ... important policy measures are not adopted, or adopted only in sub-optimal form (Weale 1996: 595).

Therefore to understand these decisions, it is essential to look at the bargains reached within and between the institutions and the ability of interests to lobby the EU.

The use of QMV for most types of environmental policy is important, but despite the leader/laggard distinction, there appear to be no fixed coalitions. Also, despite QMV, the Council tends to prefer 'consensus at (almost) any cost' (Peterson and Bomberg 1999: 58). To reduce the risk of countries coming out as clear losers, a variety of consensus-building measures are employed. These include granting exemptions or extended periods to comply with legislation to 'laggard' states. A classic example of this method was the 1997 Directive that set limits on the benzene and sulphur content of fuel. The poorer southern states were allowed to apply looser standards if they could prove that their limited crude oil supplies made it difficult to respect the agreed rules. Another way of minimizing 'losses' for states is to package a variety of deals together. For example, two separate directives on emissions were linked and German ministers made concessions on auto emission standards to secure agreement on large industrial plant emission standards (Peterson and Bomberg 1999: 185-86). These deals are clearly important in generating policy proposals, but it has also been suggested that they prevent EU environmental policy developing in anything less than an incremental manner (Baker 1997: 101-102).

Three factors are important when looking at decisions reached at the systemic level: first, the increase in veto players; secondly, the growth of EP powers; and finally, the role of the Commission as agenda setter (Peterson and Bomberg 1999: 188). Prior to the SEA the number of veto players, the actors whose agreement was needed for a change in policy, was small. The exclusion of the EP and other third parties meant the Council and Commission decided environmental policy. Post-SEA, the number of veto players has increased, with the EP beginning to play an increasingly important role. For example, the 1989 Auto Emission Directive is seen to be important, as the EP was able to force the Council to accept standards well above those preferred by most member states (Weale 1999: 46). One of the most visible signs of growing EP power can be found in the influence of its Environment Committee. Its pressure contributed to the improvement of EU rules on bathing water, urban wastewater treatment and stationary air pollution. The extension of the EP's powers by both the TEU and the Treaty of Amsterdam have extended its role as a veto-player in environmental policy, leading Weale to claim that 'it has more influence on environmental measures than is typically true for more well-established national parliaments' (Weale 1999: 37). This view is criticized by those who believe that its role has been exaggerated, as EP bargaining has often resulted in important changes only to the margins of policy proposals (Peterson and Bomberg 1999: 188).

Despite the fact that both the EP and the Council of Ministers have some powers to initiate policy, in the environmental field the right mainly lies with the Commission. As a result it tends to provide the strongest policy leadership. Throughout the development of environmental policy the Commission has acted as a policy entrepreneur, pushing its competencies to the limit and allowing the EU to develop a significant body of legislation without a formal treaty base. It would, however, be wrong to see the Commission as a unitary actor, due to the strong vertical lines of division, which help fragment the different parts of the administration (Butt Philip 1998: 266). Each Directorate General (DG) often finds it difficult to see beyond the limits of its competence, and research suggests that these competencies are jealously guarded (see Bulmer 1994: 361). The desire to support a functional constituency can lead to the criticism of tunnel vision. For example, DG Environment, which is responsible for environmental matters, is often seen as too green:

> These DG Environment people are like the Trappist monks who make
> Chimay Blea (a strong Belgium beer). They don't consult with anyone

> beside their religious patrons and they cook up very strong stuff, which
> will always appeal to a certain segment of the 'beer-drinking public'.
> They don't ever think about what a ferocious hangover is induced by the
> stuff they cook up (Peterson 1995: 482).

Likewise, many in DG Environment argue that those in DG Agriculture
do not wish to talk about the environmental problems caused by the
CAP (Weale 1996: 608). These divisions, as shall be shown, have
major implications for the EU's strategy for sustainable development.

Shaping Policy: The Sub-systemic Level
Policy-shaping decisions do not decide EU policy, rather they deter-
mine policy details or what policy options will be considered. They
occur early in the process when policy is being formulated, often before
the formal legislative process has begun. This pre-legislative stage is
where most lobbying occurs, as once political agreement emerges the
process can become inflexible. For example, it has been estimated that
once the Commission has tabled a proposal, 'scope for changing the
proposal only exists at the margins, involving about 20 per cent of the
total proposal' (Peterson and Bomberg 1999: 21). Therefore the
Commission tries to forge consensus among different actors to ensure
support before tabling a proposal, a classic element of the Monnet
method.

The sub-systemic level in environmental policy making has been
characterized as a 'messy network', where a variety of different actors
attempt to fit into the policy game (Peterson and Bomberg 1999: 192).
As a result, policy shaping tends to take place within loose issue networks. Technical expertise is an important entry card for most policy
networks, as they provide useful (and cheap) information to decision-
takers, and the environment is no exception (Greenwood 1997: 192).
Environmental policy often involves highly technical discussions
among scientists, which can make it difficult for NGOs to take part.

To ensure successful lobbying, it is important that one 'umbrella'
group speaks for all. This results from the fact that the Commission
wants to minimize the time they spend in discussions with different
groups. This means it can be difficult for green pressure groups as they
can lack homogeneity and can find it difficult to construct a common
position, although Greenwood argues that, on the whole, the main
pressure groups lobbying at EU level work well together (Rucht 1993:
87-88; Greenwood 1997).

Far more of a problem for these groups is the fact that trade and industry groups are able to dominate access. For example, a detailed study of the Packaging Waste Directive found that in the period 1990–93, 279 lobbying organizations contacted the Commission over the issue. Of these representations, 70% were from trade and industry sources, 15% were from government departments, 8% were from research institutes, and only 5% were from environmentalists, consumers or trade unions (in Greenwood 1997: 183-84). The same study concluded that the balance of this Directive reflected the greater influence of these business groups. This is despite the fact that DG Environment is seen to be one of the most open and pluralistic DGs. The problem for environmental groups is the lack of funds and the resulting lack of personnel. Despite the Commission helping to subsidize the 'Group of Eight', their financial resources are no match for those of the main industry lobbyists. The main way this lack of money affects these groups is via lack of staff. The largest pressure group, the European Environmental Bureau (EEB) had 11 staff in 1996, while the smallest, Transport and Environment only had one and a half to lobby on all environmental issues. In comparison, the Oil Companies European Organization for Environmental and Health Protection had 13 staff dedicated to environmental issues related to oil production (Greenwood 1997: 184).

EU Environmental Policy: An Assessment

It is clear that EU environmental policy has developed incrementally from 'incidental' measures towards a fully fledged policy, or as Weale succinctly puts it, 'from silence to salience within thirty years' (Weale 1999: 40). This development also meant that there has been a 'massive shift in power from nation states to the EU' in the environmental policy field (Christie 1999: 27). This change is mainly the work of the Commission, which skilfully exploited its powers and the lack of scrutiny from member states, to introduce environmental policy 'by stealth' (Weale 1999: 37). Having examined the development of EU environmental policy and the way decisions are made, it is important to assess the nature of the policies.

Baker (1997) distinguishes between two types of environmental policy:

1. Policies that have as their goal the management of environmental quality within the context of existing economic, political and

social policy and that require marginal, incremental adjustments to
the features of those policies.
2. Policies that have more radical goals, such as the reorganization of
consumption patterns, the redefinition of what constitutes economic activity, the redistribution and radical altering of Western use
of resources and the reform of the existing political and military
structures.

She argues that EU environmental policy making is characterized by
incrementalism, as shown by the various deals struck to accommodate
the leader/laggard division, which acts as a brake on the development
of radically new policies. Therefore, she concludes that the EU has
developed a weak understanding of sustainable development:

> Incrementalism makes the chances of successful translation of the
> commitment to sustainable development into actual policy dependent
> upon the extent to which the required policy changes can be fitted with
> existing policy commitments. Policy proposals that fit with the strategy
> of environmental quality management stand a greater chance of
> acceptance, while policies that fit more closely with the second, more
> radical, pattern have little, if any, chance of success. The concept of
> sustainable development has been interpreted by the Union (and its
> member states) to fit within the confines of managerial as opposed to
> radical policy solutions (Baker 1997: 102).

This lack of radical policy solutions can be seen as a result of the set of
conflicting tensions EU environmental policy embodies. On the one
hand, there are tensions between competing policy priorities (developing environmental protection or preserving internal market policies),
while on the other, there is the tension concerning the ultimate location
of these competencies (national or supranational level) (Cichowski
1998: 389). The EU has to manage these competing priorities in order
to create policy. As has been shown, the development of EU environmental policy has been characterized by the conflict between preserving
the environment and preserving the free trade policies essential for the
success of the single market. This conflict is evident in the Treaties (the
use of Article 95 or 175), national policy and ECJ rulings (the Danish
bottle case) and even relations between DGs (DG Environment and the
'economic' DGs). For example, it is argued that in the main 'economic'
DGs, a neo-liberal ethos is discernible, whereas DG Environment is
infused with preferences for ecological modernization (Rosamund
2000: 120). Combined with the dispute over which is the most appro-

priate level for environmental policy (the subsidiarity principle), it is unsurprising that managerial rather than radical solutions tend to emerge from the EU.

Linking back to Dryzek's classification, it is possible to argue that, on the whole, EU environmental policy has so far reflected a reformist relationship with industrialism, with the EU promoting 'prosaic' policies. This 'environmental problem solving' discourse is evident within the EU's focus upon regulating pollution levels and combating the negative environmental externalities caused by the single market project.

This has led many green groups to criticize EU environmental policy for being too wedded to what they consider to be an outdated discourse that fails to accept the importance of a widespread reorganization of society to prevent environmental meltdown. They also argue that large economic interests, which prevent any shift to these new discourses, have captured the EU. Since the fifth EAP and the Treaty of Amsterdam, however, the EU has committed itself to a 'sustainability discourse', with its plans to incorporate sustainability into all policy areas. Whether this has replaced the environmental problem-solving discourse and to what extent it has been a success will be examined in more detail in Chapter 5. The developing co-decision powers of the EP in this area may increase the influence of 'outsider' national green actors in the EU policy process. The other scenario is that the business lobby begins to take the EP more seriously and use their greater resources to increase their access to MEPs. Increasing the powers of the EP could also be seen as decreasing the democratic deficit within the EU, although it does not go far enough to counter the criticisms levelled at EU democracy by many green actors. For instance, unanimity is still required for those measures that some member states regard as a policy step too far, especially fiscal policy. The green lobby would see measures such as an EU carbon tax, although still within the industrialization discourse, as a crucial step towards making a significant reduction in EU pollution levels, although this must also be seen in the light of the differing views of member states to the issue of the environment. With member states like Spain opposed to radical EU measures, the Amsterdam compromises can be seen as a small victory for the environmental lobby.

4 |

Raising the Environmental Standard: The Emergence of Green Actors in the European Union

> [E]nvironmentalists have confronted a Union that, with the exception of
> the European Council, has shown itself to be both attitudinally sympa-
> thetic and structurally open to the interests of the movement (Marks and
> McAdam 1996: 269).

As with national political systems, surrounding any policy field within
the EU one can identify a broad set of interest groups and lobbyists
seeking to gain influence over the direction of policy development.
Chapter 3 has already highlighted the many different channels within
the EU institutions through which it is possible to seek effective influence and action. Within the environmental sphere, interest group activity plays a key role in shaping the direction and style of EU policy.

As environmental issues have gained a greater role at EU level, and
EU policy making in this field has grown in significance, so the pattern
of movements and actors seeking to shape EU environmental policy has
subsequently expanded. Indeed a full, detailed identification and analysis of the activities of all of the many different interest groups active
within the environmental sphere would require a book in itself. In
seeking to provide a taste of this complex tapestry of interest group
activity, this chapter focuses predominantly upon the representation and
influence of the major green actors at EU level. Obviously these groups
cannot be viewed in isolation from the broader activities of alternative
lobby groups active within the environmental sphere. Examining the
activities of the green actors will therefore inevitably highlight the
important influence of other alternative actors upon the direction and
pace of environmental policy making.

Since the 1970s the environmental movement has emerged as a significant political force within a number of European countries. Move-

ments such as FoE and Greenpeace have seen membership rise steadily and have become established features of the political scene across Europe. More recently, smaller and more radical organizations, focused upon direct-action campaigning around issues such as animal rights, road building, genetically modified (GM) foods and more broadly global capitalism, have added a more informal and more loosely organized dimension to environmental protest. In addition to the actions of environmental protest groups, the rise and success of green parties across Europe has provided further evidence of the public's concern for environmental issues. The advent of direct elections to the EP in 1979 led to the emergence of a small but vociferous green group, raising questions over the environmental record of the Union and its member states. The actions of both the green parties and the environmental movements have played a major role in forcing green issues onto national political agendas and subsequently onto the political agenda of the EU.

This chapter examines the way in which the green lobby has attempted to gain an influential voice at EU level. It seeks to paint a broad picture of the environmental network active at EU level by identifying the key actors and assessing the extent to which these groups have successfully adapted to lobbying processes within the Union. It examines the opportunities and constraints facing those seeking more effective forms of environmental policy making from within what has primarily been an economic Union. It also identifies some of the primary barriers and debates which pose significant problems to the effective coordination of environmental interests at EU level.

The chapter focuses upon three main channels through which green issues are highlighted. It examines the lobbying role of environmental movements, the parliamentary role of the GGEP, and the emerging, and potentially influential, role of the EEA. As well as examining the work of those actors which have established themselves in Brussels, the chapter also reflects upon the role of the national environmental movements. A critical analysis of the actions of these groups provides an overall picture of the strengths and weaknesses of the environmental lobby at the EU level, and questions whether or not the picture presented by Marks and McAdam, at the beginning of this chapter, of a 'sympathetic' and 'open' European Union reflects the experiences of the movement itself.

The Significance of Movement Mobilization at EU Level

A number of explanations can be identified as to why environmental movements should seek to encompass the EU level within their frame of activism. First, it is suggested that, theoretically at least, environmental movements should be well suited to supranational action, given that the need to act beyond purely national interests is a vital dimension of the green critique of modern society. As mentioned earlier, the heart of the environmental debate concerns the claim that environmental damage represents an international concern, not simply a national one. As such, it is impossible to consider issues of environmental protection and control within purely national boundaries. The centrality of the need for international cooperation and agreement places the EU as a significant focal point for action. Environmental actors, similarly, can potentially tackle international concerns and broad environmental issues which they find difficult to effectively address at a purely national level and which require broad international action.

A second argument for an EU focus to environmental action concerns the growing impact of EU policy on national political agendas. It is argued that, as with other areas of policy, as the EU's environmental agenda has expanded a greater number of decisions and environmental standards are being set at EU level rather than at national level. If, as seems the case, this pattern is set to continue, and power over environmental policy is shifting beyond national governments, it is logical for the environmental movements to undertake a similar transition and follow this flow of power (see Pollack 2000).

The nature of the policy process at EU level has also played a significant role in encouraging environmental movements to locate in Brussels. The EU policy process represents a relatively open channel for environmental interests. With the environmental sphere being a relatively recent expansion to the EU's policy competencies, groups are still seeking to solidify themselves as key sources of information and influence for EU decision-making institutions. Lowe and Ward, for example, identify the EU environmental policy sector as being characterized by 'loose unstable policy networks, easily penetrated by environmentalists' (Lowe and Ward 1998: 156). Similarly, direct elections to the EP provided an early opportunity for a number of national green parties, such as those in France and Germany, to gain parliamentary representation where they had often been sidelined at national level.

The discovery that some aspects of the EU appear to provide a more flexible and open attitude towards green issues has therefore been encouraging for environmental groups, especially when compared to the relatively 'closed' political systems that operate within a number of the EU's member states. Focusing upon the EU has been particularly beneficial to those environmental groups active within countries where they have been largely isolated from the policy process. McCormick highlights the case of Britain as one such example, stating that:

> because the British government has made few concessions on domestic issues, British environmental groups have increasingly seen Brussels as a court of redress and a means of out-manoeuvring the government (McCormick 1991: 132-33).

Environmental groups have therefore been able to identify within the EU structures a potential set of opportunities for access and influence, beyond those which they are capable of utilizing at national levels.

The impetus for developing an effective environmental lobby in Brussels has not solely come from within the environmental groups themselves, however. As green issues have appeared on the political agenda, members of key EU institutions have also been keen to identify themselves as 'receptive' to environmental issues and debates. In attempting to 'green' the EU, both the Commission and the EP have, on occasions, actively encouraged contact with the environmental movements. Lowe and Ward (1998: 156) suggest that the process reflects the desire on the part of some EU officials to encourage a counter-lobby to combat the influence of the powerful business and agricultural lobby groups active at EU level.

The impetus clearly exists, therefore, to encourage the growth of an effective environmental lobby in Brussels. However, one must be careful not to homogenize the EU. This apparent openness is not evident throughout all EU bodies and institutions, raising important questions concerning the receptiveness of the EU to environmental protest. In assessing the role and development of the various environmental actors, many barriers will be identified which have restricted the extent to which these groups have really been able to successfully seize the potential opportunities available to them.

Environmental Campaigning in the EU

The first thing that strikes anybody examining the environmental lobby in Brussels is that it is constantly in a state of flux. Due to the broad reach of environmental concerns, it is difficult to identify a consistent set of actors within the environmental policy field. Groups have a tendency to move in and out of this policy field depending upon the issue under consideration. In her analysis of the green movement in the European Union, Bomberg recognizes this complexity, stating that:

> EU policy-making incorporates a wide range of decision-making centres and a diverse array of actors who move in and out of policy arenas and have different views of desired policy outcomes. Compared with other EU policy sectors, environmental policy features relatively ad hoc policy-making structures in which not only a large, but to a certain extent unpredictable number of conflicting interests participate (Bomberg 1998: 44).

Despite this ambiguity, however, it is possible to identify a set of central players and developments to which one can ascribe a primary role in the emergence of environmental concerns at EU level. As with the issue itself, environmental groups are relative latecomers to the lobbying activities of the EU and have been fairly slow in making their presence felt. The gradual increase in activity, however, has seen a broadening of green representation. This representation ranges from umbrella organizations to Brussels-based branches of international movements, to parliamentary parties and also information and resource centres. In addition, national movements also see the EU as a potential source of redress against governments who fail to maintain environmental standards. Marks and McAdam suggest that: 'the lobby is comprised of four major organisations, several lesser groups, and at least half a dozen specialised environmental networks' (1995: 269).

The Role of the Environmental Movements

Environmental movements represent today a significant pressure upon EU policy makers. However, the emerging role of these movements in Brussels has been a relatively recent phenomenon. As mentioned in Chapter 2, the EU has been viewed with scepticism by many within the environmental movement, often being perceived as part of the problem rather than a potential source of influence and change. This scepticism was a strong factor in the late arrival of the environmental lobby. While a broad and diverse range of national movements and networks have now begun to see the EU as a significant campaigning focus, the environmental lobby located in Brussels focuses largely around a central group of key organizations.

For much of the 1970s and 1980s the EEB represented the only significant environmental organization in Brussels (Lowe and Goyder 1983). The EEB was founded in 1974, coinciding with the initiation of the first EAP, with the intention of providing an umbrella organization with the purpose of representing the interests of environmental NGOs across Europe in Brussels. It has since played a major role in getting the environment accepted as one of the spheres of responsibility of the EU, and as such acted as a catalyst to encourage other movements to recognize the EU as a valuable focus for green action and to create organizations to lobby at this level. The EEB outlines its objectives as:

> to bring together environmental non-governmental organisations in the member states in order to strengthen their effect and impact on the environmental policy and projects of the European Union (EEB website, accessed 8 May 2001).

Although only 25 organizations were affiliated to the EEB when it began, membership has grown consistently so that it now represents 130 NGOs from 24 countries including all 15 EU member states. Rucht estimates that the EEB represents over eight million people across the EU countries (Rucht 1993: 83). The EEB is in a distinctive position among the environmental lobby in the EU. It was established and funded by the EU and is recognized by DG Environment as the only representative organization. Because the Commission recognizes its expertise in environmental affairs in this way, the EEB is often able to gain greater access to the Commission and has, therefore, a potentially significant starting point from which to try and influence policy.

David (1994) suggest that the historical evolution of the activities of the EEB can be divided into three key stages. First, the EEB focused upon highlighting the connection between the development of the EU and the need for effective environmental policy. This represented a dual process of attempting to get EU decision-making institutions to recognize the relevance of the environment as a key policy on the one hand, while also attempting to demonstrate to environmental groups the potential significance of EU institutions and policy making to their actions, on the other. Secondly, the EEB had to act as a focal point for enhancing the environmental movements' abilities to act as a Europe-wide network, given that most groups operated at either local or national levels only. The third stage identified by David is the requirement of the EEB to come to terms with the widening agenda and the broadening of the Union into a major international institution (David

1994). Clearly therefore, the EEB has been at the centre of much of the transition towards an effective environmental lobby at EU level.

Despite its relative significance to the environmental field, however, its strength and role is still relatively limited. The EEB has few full-time staff members and generally lacks the resources that are available to other organizations active at EU level. This is a resource problem which afflicts much of the activities of the environmental movement. Rucht places the EEB in perspective, claiming that it has

> less money and staff than a medium-sized national environmental group
> in Great Britain, Germany or the Netherlands (Rucht 1993: 87).

It is also suggested that the EEB's actual role falls some way short of the European lobby organization that was initially envisaged. Many of the NGOs that are members of the EEB view its significance and role more in terms of a facilitator for information provision and exchange between organizations, rather than utilizing it as a lobbying vehicle for broad European objectives. The limited resources available to many of these organizations results in them focusing predominantly on national issues and concerns rather than seeking action on broad campaigns, which are not viewed as so immediate. The EEB's reliance on EU funding has also been criticized by some environmental campaigners. In particular, it has faced criticism from green party activists who see it as an institutionalized organization set up by the Commission and posing no significant threat or challenge to the status quo within the EU.

In the 1980s, international environmental organizations sought to create offices in Brussels, creating a caucus of movement organizations. Environmental lobbying at the EU level increased significantly with the arrival of three major environmental organizations in Brussels in the late 1980s. Greenpeace International established an office in Brussels in 1988. Greenpeace is one of the best-known international environmental organizations with offices in approximately 25 countries worldwide, and a reputation for utilizing unconventional, direct action techniques which have raised both media and public attention to environmental issues. FoE represent a similar form of direct action movement, focusing on environmental issues that were often ignored by government officials such as those surrounding nuclear power, industrial pollution and quality of life issues (see Dalton 1994). Although initially based in the United States, European branches emerged during the 1970s. An EU-based office was established in 1986.

The third international environmental organization with an established base in Brussels is the WWF. The WWF is an older organization with its roots firmly within the conservation community and a tradition of fairly conventional political activity. A change of name from the original World Wildlife Fund reflected a transition within the organization as it sought to broaden its focus and tactics, adding to its mission statement the goals of 'sustainable use of natural resources and the reduction of pollution and wasteful resource consumption' (in Bomberg 1998: 23). The establishment in 1989 of a Brussels office, which focused specifically upon EU issues, represented one aspect of this expansion of WWF's activities.

The establishment of Brussels offices by these three major environmental organizations provided added impetus for greater coordination of the environmental lobby. In combination with the EEB these movements initially became known as the 'gang of four'. Greater coordination enabled the movements to strengthen their position, gaining a closer working relationship with the head of the NGO liaison unit in DG Environment. In addition, all except Greenpeace received financial assistance from the liaison unit. In an attempt to influence as broad a public as possible with a relatively meagre set of resources, the groups developed common policy statements and campaigns where it was clear that the interests of the movements overlapped and that a broader scale campaign would be more effective. Similarly, each movement took responsibility for certain aspects of environmental campaigning and lobbying, rather than having each group tackling similar issues individually. In line with this process, the WWF has often taken the lead on issues surrounding Structural Funds, while the EEB has placed more of a focus upon tackling pollution issues (Bomberg 1998: 134).

This more coherent and coordinated approach to environmental campaigning at EU level was further expanded with the participation of four further specialist networks: Climate Network Europe; the European Federation for Transport and Environment; International Friends of Nature; and Birdlife International. As their names suggest, these organizations have a much more specific agenda focus than the broader environmental organizations discussed above and provided a useful specialist knowledge base for the environmental lobby. From the mid-1990s, therefore, the original 'gang of four' expanded to include these four additional organizations, and have often been referred to as the 'Green G8' (see Table 4.1). The groups hold regular meetings and have

Table 4.1. The Green G8: A Brief Guide

Organization	Activities
Birdlife International	Developed from the International Council for Bird Preservation, Birdlife International was created in 1993 to focus upon policy work as well as scientific research. Birdlife has nearly 2 million members and more than 100 affiliated organizations around the world including one from each EU member state.
Climate Network Europe (CNE)	Created in 1989 CNE is the focal point for 78 NGOs in Western Europe working upon climate-related concerns. Activities focused primarily upon lobbying, identifying itself as an 'information link' to national member organizations.
Greenpeace	Greenpeace has national offices in 29 countries, as well as 3 multinational offices. Membership is approximately 2.9 million. Activities focus upon a broad array of environmental issues, utilizing numerous pressure tactics including direct action as well as policy research.
European Environmental Bureau (EEB)	Created in 1974 to inform environmental organizations of relevant policy developments at EU level and to provide a lobbying voice for these groups, the EEB has 135 member organizations in 23 countries.
Friends of the Earth Europe (FoEE)	Created in 1986 as an EU coordinating body for FoE members. Part of the broader international FoE organization which boasts approximately 900,000 members. Activities range from large-scale direct action campaigns to localized lobbying. Identified as the largest network of environmental organizations working at grassroots level in Europe.
International Friends of Nature (IFN)	Developed from conservation movements of the late nineteenth century, the IFN's primary focus is 'ecological tourism' the protection of the natural environment and the encouragement of sustainable development. Based predominantly in Europe, IFN has a membership of approximately 600,000 and operates in 11 of the EU member states.
European Federation for Transport and Environment (T&E)	Established in 1989 to provide an umbrella organization for NGO activities surrounding transport, the T&E has 37 member organizations and utilizes its network of experts to provide scientific research and 'proactive and constructive' policy solutions.
World Wide Fund for Nature (WWF)	Formed in 1961 WWF has been most widely recognized for its work on wildlife preservation. Recent years have witnessed a broadening in the organization's focus, encompassing more broad-ranging environmental issues. The WWF has 4.7 million supporters worldwide, of which 3 million are from Europe. In the Netherlands more than one person per household is believed to be a WWF supporter.

Source: Details on organizations are taken from *Environment for Europeans: Magazine of the Directorate-General for the Environment,* No. 3, July 2000, pp. 5-8.

produced a number of combined policy papers, strengthening their claims beyond what could be achieved by any of the groups individually. The increased pressure and influence of the environmental movements was seen to have paid dividends with the creation of the General Consultative Forum on the Environment (more generally known as the Green Forum).[1] This provided a forum through which a broad range of interested parties could be consulted and advise the Commission on environmental policy development. Its membership included not only the NGOs, but also representatives from industry, business, local authorities, trade unions and academia.

Problems and Barriers Facing Environmental NGOs at EU Level

At first glance, therefore, there would seem to be strong evidence to suggest that the environmental movement is emerging as a significant force at EU level. The growth in organizational presence and lobbying activities, the level of access to DG Environment achieved by the movements and the increase in EU environmental policy all point towards a successful process of interest mobilization and a fairly significant level of influence. Indeed, Lowe and Ward suggest that the environmentalists have succeeded in producing a relatively unified European voice from which to challenge pre-existing attitudes towards environmental policy. They suggest that this reflects not only a lower degree of competition among environmental organizations compared to other lobby groups but also 'a practical response to dealing with issues that cross national borders' (Lowe and Ward 1998: 156). Similarly, Bomberg argues that the relatively open style of policy making in the environmental sphere has proved positive for outside groups such as the environmental NGOs seeking to gain an influence. She suggests that:

> in a number of cases, NGOs have been able to secure the enactment of environmental regulatory policies stricter than those achieved at the national level (Bomberg 1998: 128).

Despite this progression, however, the status of the environmental movement in many ways remains relatively marginal to the policy process in the EU. While they have undoubtedly made great strides, a

---

1. The Green Forum's title was later extended to the General Consultative Forum on the Environment and Sustainable Development as the concept of sustainability gained greater significance to EU policy making.

number of barriers continue to restrict the abilities of the movements to gaining effective influence.

At the heart of the problems facing the environmental movement is the question of resources. The environmental movement is significantly understaffed and under-resourced, both in comparison to other lobby groups active at EU level but also in relation to the national environmental movements which they seek to support and represent. Long suggests that environmental groups find it difficult to marshall the resources and skills which are clearly available at national level, to be able to have a really effective impact upon the decision-making process in Brussels (Long 1998: 117). The EU level organizations that have been outlined above generally lack the strength and active support that the national sections of the same organizations are able to attain. For example, Greenpeace has been reluctant to fund its EU organization as effectively as the national organizations.

Rucht suggests that Greenpeace has proved to be a reluctant lobbyist at EU level partly because the nature and style of Greenpeace's activities put it at odds with the EU policy process. He suggests that Greenpeace finds it difficult to adapt to the task of lobbying and negotiating with EU bureaucrats and that 'the very idea of doing this kind of unspectacular work with and within bureaucracies does not really correspond to the philosophy of Greenpeace' (Rucht 1993: 85-86). A similar reluctance is evident with regard to the resources provided by national groups to EU activities. Lowe and Ward's (1998) study of British environmental movements, for example, indicated that although most of the movements recognized the EU as a significant channel for environmental policy, very few actually had a designated European Officer.

Additionally, the green agenda is not the sole property of environmental movements. Many other sets of interests compete to influence the level of environmental regulation emerging from the EU. The gap in resources is even more noticeable when comparing those available to the environmental movement with those of other EU lobby groups attempting to influence the extent and direction of EU environmental policy. Rucht highlights this divide within the field of biotechnology. Within this sphere, he claims:

> whereas the environmental groups in Brussels can rely on only one full-time expert in this field, the biotechnology group is backed by a strong industrial lobby, the Senior Advisory Board on Biotechnology, which is

sponsored by 31 firms (among them giants such as Bayer, Ciba-Geigy, DuPont and Unilever) and has access to an array of expertise (Rucht 1993: 89).

A similar picture appears to confront the environmental movements in many of the spheres of policy making. While the environmental movements must seek to rationalize the use of resources across a broad range of policy spheres they are persistently confronted with a much more professional lobbying opposition with specialist knowledge and interests. Thus the example of the biotechnology sphere is mirrored in other aspects. For example, the Chemical Industry Federation possesses a permanent staff of 70, and has 4000 persons from its member companies and associations involved in its expert committees (Grant 1993: 12).

This numerical and financial barrier proves even more restrictive when one considers that DG Environment, although the focus for much environmental policy making and lobbying, actually represents only one focal point in the lobbying process. It is also, as Chapter 3 noted, a relatively marginal focal point when compared to the more powerful DGs, such as those focusing upon industry, agriculture and technology. As mentioned, the nature of environmental issues and problems cut across many sectors of policy making within the EU. Restricting the lobbying process to policy emerging from within the DG Environment can, therefore, risk missing key developments from other aspects of EU policy that may have a significant environmental concern. The green lobby is forced to spread its resources across a broader canopy, covering a myriad of different lobbying points. In doing so it faces the challenge of influencing policy networks that are much less responsive to its position than DG Environment, and far less willing to include environmental organizations in the decision-making process. As will be discussed in detail in Chapter 5, there is an increasing emphasis upon sustainable development within the EU's fifth and sixth EAPs. This has resulted in greater emphasis being placed upon the need to consider environmental factors in all aspects of EU policy making. While this may represent a positive step in the broader consideration of environmental concerns within the EU, it undoubtedly places further pressure on the limited resources available to the environmental movements in their attempts to influence policy.

Given the competition for policy influence at EU level, it is hardly surprising that despite what appears to be a relatively encouraging relationship with DG Environment, the environmental movements find it persistently difficult to gain substantial influence over the policy-making process. McCormick draws similar conclusions, suggesting that 'industry has considerably more influence over the legislative process' than the environmental NGOs. The result of this imbalance, he argues, is that 'EU environmental law and policy reflects more fully the priorities of corporate Europe than it does of NGOs' (McCormick 1999: 203).

While national environmental groups strengthen their position in a number of EU member states, the ability to coordinate these forces effectively at European level remains relatively problematic. Unifying a disparate green movement is not, however, a problem restricted to the EU level. National environmental movements have similarly struggled, and often actively resisted, attempts to create a unified and coordinated national umbrella organization. As Lowe and Ward suggest, the environmental movement at EU level has a tendency to exacerbate these difficulties as they

> reproduce at a transnational level the problems experienced by national umbrella organisations but with the added problems of having to overcome differences in the participants' cultural and national backgrounds (Lowe and Ward 1998: 91).

Environmental movements continue to remain relatively autonomous in their actions and lack the homogeneity of many other forms of pressure/interest group. In many cases, groups have often tended to favour co-ordinated action on an ad hoc, issue-centred basis, rather than seeking to create a formalized organizational process. The primary focus for interaction between environmental movements has on many occasions centred upon the sharing of information, and this appears to again be reflected in the manner in which national member groups have sought to utilize the EEB. For many national movements, EU action centres upon ensuring national governments enforce EU regulations and standards, rather than broader international campaigning and lobbying. In this sense, one could argue that the movement's successes are largely based upon being 'reactive' during the implementation stage rather than being 'proactive' in policy instigation and construction.

This lack of homogeneity both within and between the environmental movements at the EU level often makes it difficult to develop a common stance. As mentioned above, this difficulty reflects not only the differing priorities of the individual movements but also the national differences between groups. The aims and objectives of the movements can often reflect the differing national commitments to environmental protection. Rucht's analysis suggests that with the exception of the United Kingdom (where there is an active environmental movement despite a weak commitment to the environment from the state), the objectives of the national environmental movements reflect the pattern of commitment to environmental issues from the respective member states. This diversity, he argues, produces an array of attitudes from within the various national environmental movements to the development of EU policy making.

> Whereas the leading group is fiercely fighting for restrictive standards [in the EU] and sometimes fears that, with new EC regulations, the situation in the home country could worsen, the rearguard is often satisfied with moderate standards which well surpass what has been achieved so far back home (Rucht 1993: 88).

In summarizing the position of the environmental movements in relation to the EU, it would appear that they face a significant dilemma. Given that these movements possess a relatively limited set of resources, in terms of both finance and personnel, they must decide whether these resources can best be utilized at national or EU level. While the EU, and in particular DG Environment, represents a significant focal point for the development of environmental policy, the lack of resources means that the environmental lobby struggles to compete with the more organized and highly funded European lobby groups. This often results in the movements gaining relatively little input into environmental policy making. While this situation continues, national environmental movements remain reluctant to commit valuable resources to EU campaigning, especially if they are able to gain greater influence and impact at national level.

The Role of Green Parties in the European Parliament

The advent of direct elections to the European Parliament in 1979, provided an alternative channel through which to seek a 'green voice' at EU level. Green parties emerged throughout Europe during the 1980s and 1990s as a challenge to conventional party politics. Their distinctiveness was seen to extend beyond purely the 'new politics' of environmentalism but was also reflected within the 'anti-partyist' and decentralized party organizations and the critique of the increasing 'professionalization' and centralization of party politics (see Poguntke 1987; Müller-Rommel 1989; Kitschelt 1988). Initially gaining success at local and regional level, the emergence of the green parties as a significant political force was further enhanced by the breakthrough of a number of parties into their respective national parliaments. In the late 1990s, a number of green parties gained coalition roles within national governments, signifying a crucial breakthrough for the greens.

During this period, elections to the EP have played a significant part in helping to enforce the political credibility of the European green parties. The European elections have often provided green parties with an initial opportunity to demonstrate their effectiveness as parliamentary actors as it has on a number of occasions provided less of an electoral barrier than elections to national assemblies. Although no green parties gained seats in the first direct elections in 1979, by 1984 increased support resulted in 11 green MEPs being elected from three European countries (Bomberg 1998: 90). This trend continued throughout the 1980s and 1990s as the GGEP expanded and incorporated representatives from a broader range of nationalities. Following the 1999 European Parliamentary elections, the GGEP constituted 6% of the parliamentary members, and contained representatives from 11 EU member states. Table 4.2 charts the continuing expansion of green party representation within the EP. In most cases, it is interesting to note that the levels of green party support across member states is largely reflective of the 'leader/laggard' split highlighted in earlier chapters. Two cases stand out as interesting exceptions, however. In both Denmark and the United Kingdom (until 1999) green parties failed to make a parliamentary breakthrough, but in both cases green parties have played 'second fiddle' to strong and effective environmental movements who have largely captured the green agenda. In Denmark, a high level of commitment to environmental issues by parties of the left has further weakened the role of the greens.

Although fluctuations in support have altered the balance between the various European green parties the overall pattern within the GGEP has been one of expansion as a parliamentary force. The GGEP has developed an expanding role in attempting to influence and shape policy at EU level. It now has at least one member sitting on every European Parliamentary Committee and has secured more than one seat on those committees which it identified as of particular significance. These included the environment, energy and the institutional commit-

Table 4.2. The Emergence of Green Parties in the European Parliament

Green party	1984		1989		1994		1999	
	Vote (%)	MEPs	Vote (%)	MEPs	Vote (%)	MEPs	Vote (%)	MEPs
Austria (*Die Grünen*)					6.8	1	9.2	2
Belgium (*Ecolo*)	9.9	1	16.6	2	6.7	1	7.5	2
(*Agalev*)	7.1	1	12.2	1	4.8	1	8.4	3
Finland (*Vihreä Liitto*)			-	-	7.6	1	13.4	2
France (*Les Verts*)	3.4	0	10.6	9	4.9	0	9.7	9
Germany (*Bündnis 90/Die Grünen*)	8.2		8.4	8	10.1	12	6.4	7
Ireland (*Comhaontas Glas*)			3.8	0	7.9	2	6.7	2
Italy (*Federazione dei Verdi*)	-	-	6.2	7	3.2	3	1.8	2
Luxembourg (*Dei Greng*)			6.1	0	10.9	1	10.7	1
Netherlands (*Groen Links*)	5.6	2	7	2	3.7	1	11.9	4
Spain (*Los Verdes*)			1.9	1	0.7	0	1.4	0
Sweden (*Miljöpartiet de Gröna*)	-	-	-	-	17.2	4	9.5	2
United Kingdom (The Green Party)		0	14.9	0	3.2	0	6.3	2

Source: Statistics taken from Federation of European Green Parties' website. Also see Carter 1994.

tees (Bomberg 1998: 145). The success and activism of the European green parties at both national and EU levels is often seen as an important factor in the increasing significance attached to environmental policy in the EU.

In recent years, changes within the EU have increased the power and influence of the EP. This has resulted in the Commission having to give greater consideration to the attitudes and opinions of MEPs and provided further impetus for the GGEP to actively champion the importance of environmental considerations within EU policy making. Arp (1992) estimates that the subject of the environment constituted over one-tenth of the questions asked in the EP. As well as asking questions within the EP, the GGEP have also sought alternative processes for influencing policy and highlighting the green agenda. Green MEPs have on a number of occasions conducted protest actions and hosted seminars to identify key issues and concerns.

Problems and Barriers Facing Green Parties in the EU

As with the discussion of the actions of the environmental movements earlier, despite forcing themselves firmly onto the EU's political stage, the actual impact of the actions of the green parties in the EP has been patchy. Again, closer inspection reveals a number of important barriers and pressures restricting the impact of the green parties, both practical and ideological in nature.

First, one of the central weaknesses of the GGEP's activities is that its scope has so far remained relatively narrow, focusing unsurprisingly around the EP. While this has been the obvious target for the green parties, they have failed to build any strong links with other EU decision-making institutions, in particular the Commission. This failure, Bomberg suggests, has left the GGEP relatively isolated from all aspects of the decision-making process outside the sphere of the EP. This has significant repercussions in that while green MEPs have on many occasions highlighted important issues and considerations within the Parliament, they have not been able to successfully follow this through to help shape EU policy in that field. Hence Bomberg concludes:

> If greens have had some agenda-setting influence, they have had little success in shaping policies once they have left the parliament, and almost no measurable influence over policy outcomes. Even when

successfully gaining the support of the EP, green reports and demands have often been subsequently ignored by the Commission, Council of Ministers or members states (Bomberg 1998: 148).

Secondly, the European greens have encountered a number of ideological and strategic problems similar to those encountered by national green parties across Europe. In particular, problems have been raised both regarding the ideological commitments and aims of the green parties and also regarding the relationship between the green parties and the broader environmental movements. For a number of green parties the EU represents a paradox in itself. Although potentially providing an effective forum for green issues, many parties are fundamentally at odds with the current structure and political style of the EU.

In Sweden, for example, *Miljöpartiet de Gröna* gained electoral success at both National and European elections, with an anti-EU platform (see Burchell 1996). Indeed, the 17% of the vote that *Miljöpartiet* achieved in 1995, still represents the strongest electoral performance of any of the European green parties. The Swedish greens, along with others, claim that membership of the EU entails a diluting of national environmental standards on the one hand, and a weakening of the democratic process on the other. In particular, they identify the unelected nature of the Commission and the relative weakness of the EP as key aspects of this democratic weakness. Other green parties, however, appear slightly more pragmatic about the nature of the EU. While recognizing its faults, they are keen to influence change and reform from the inside and suggest that broad environmental reform could be achieved in the future.

An additional strategic concern for the European greens is the need to work with other political groups to achieve their objectives. As at national level, there has been significant debate concerning whether green parties should remain 'true' to green principles and refuse to seek coalitions (maintaining a 'neither left or right' autonomous stance), or whether they have to act more pragmatically and accept the need to compromise to gain influence.[2] These debates have also been transposed onto the European stage, where arguably the need for cooperation and compromise is exacerbated. Despite their reluctance to compromise, to get issues raised onto the European agenda the greens have

2.   In particular see 'realo-fundis' debates within the German Green Party *Die Grünen* (Markovits and Gorski 1993; Frankland and Schoonmaker 1992) and the extension of this concept to other European green parties (Doherty 1992).

to gain support from other political groupings. This leaves the European greens with a significant dilemma. As Bomberg summarizes:

> Greens loathe such compromise because of the dilution of green princi-
> ples it implies. Moreover, going along with the larger groups often
> means that the greens' ideas are swallowed up and become indisting-
> uishable from those of the 'mainstream' parties. Yet to hold out often
> leaves the greens isolated, marginalised, and no nearer achieving their
> goals (Bomberg 1998: 141).

This dilemma has proved no easier to resolve for the greens at European level than it has at national level, and has on occasions highlighted
divisions and differences between the members of GGEP.

The third problem facing the European greens concerns their
relationship with the environmental movements. Although one might
expect a relatively strong relationship to exist between these two sets of
environmental actors, the reality is somewhat different. Despite sharing
common concerns, and the fact that both groups are fighting against
much larger and stronger adversaries, there is a relatively weak relationship between the parties and the movements at the EU level. Part of
the explanation for this again reflects the ideological question of
compromising to achieve objectives. While some of the environmental
movements have been prepared to accept compromise on a number of
occasions in an attempt to shape and influence EU policy making, this
process has alienated a number of green party activists who strongly
oppose such action. As such, the green parties have often proved reluctant to support the actions of the environmental movements, claiming
that they are too quick to compromise to gain influence within the
Commission.

As a final consideration, it is again important to recognize that the
European green parties are far from homogeneous organizations. As
such, there are open divisions between parties and quite significant
differences of opinion regarding the role of the GGEP. Similarly, the
parties also differ regarding their commitment to activism at EU level.
In particular, those countries who have failed to gain EP representation,
notably the UK Green Party until 1999, have been more reluctant to
devote limited resources to EU issues. At times this can lead to the
perception of a far from unified green party organization at the EU.

Overall, it would appear that one of the primary problems restricting
the capabilities of the green parties in the EU to influence environmental policy making, is that they constitute an alternative political

style that is ill-suited to the demands of political action within the EU. Referring back to Dryzek's categorization of environmental discourse, outlined in Chapter 2, green parties appear to seek a far more 'radical' and 'imaginative' set of changes to those which form the centre-piece for environmental policy making in the EU. As such, their standpoint appears fundamentally at odds with the broader pattern of policy development which the EU currently pursues.

Undoubtedly, the greens' reluctance to compromise has left them in a relatively marginalized position. In many cases, the policy stance of the green parties remains a long way from those of the other interested parties within the environmental policy sphere. A weak relationship with the environmental movements and a focus on the EP at the expense of engaging in a working relationship with the Commission has weakened their ability to influence strongly the direction of the EU's environmental policy agenda (Bomberg 1998: 133). That said, the greens are no strangers to finding themselves at odds with their political surroundings. In recent years, national green parties have faced important challenges which have resulted, in some cases, in reorganization and reform. As a more pragmatic and 'professionalized' attitude appears to be emerging, this may well feed into the work of the GGEP.

The Emerging Role of the European Environmental Agency

As well as the actions of the environmental movements and green parties, it is also important to consider the emerging role within EU environmental politics for the EEA. Given that environmental damage and pollution levels are a key focus for environmental policy making within the EU, it is important to get comparable, accurate information regarding the state of the environment within each of the 15 EU member states. The EEA therefore functions as an environmental resource and information centre for the EU.

The EEA was established by Council regulation in May 1990. Failure to agree to a location for the agency, however, meant that its functioning was delayed until December 1993, when it was agreed that it should be located in Copenhagen. It was claimed that the EEA would function as an information and observation network through which the EU could assess the impact of newly emerging environmental regulations. The objectives of the agency, it was stated, was to provide:

objective, reliable, and comparable information at European level, which
will enable the Community and the member states to take the requisite
measures to protect the environment and to assess the results of such
measures and to ensure that the public is properly informed about the
state of the environment (CEC 1990a cited in Wynne and Waterton
1998: 120).

Given this remit, the EEA clearly has the potential to play a significant
role within the environmental policy-making sphere, not only in
relation to the EU institutions but also in connection with the environmental lobby. The EEA has an independent management board with a
representative from each member state, members from two non-EU
states, Iceland and Norway, two representatives from the Commission
and two experts chosen by the EP. Wynne and Waterton claim that the
importance accorded to the EEA is reflected in the fact that each
member state's representative is the senior environmental policy
official in that government, and that the Commission's members are the
two most senior officials in DG Environment and DG Research
(formerly DGXII) (Wynne and Waterton 1998: 122).

The role of collating and disseminating reliable, comparable information on the environment across the EU inevitably brings the EEA into
contact with environmental movements. Potentially, therefore, the EEA
may represent an additional channel through which environmental
movements can raise issues and concerns and identify where member
states are failing to meet environmental regulations and standards. In
addition, the EEA can also be an effective source of information for the
environmental movements themselves. Lowe and Ward claim that the
EEA has the potential to develop into 'an important two-way
information channel for national environmentalists' (Lowe and Ward
1998: 159).

However, although the EEA appears to be a significant step towards a
more unified, 'reliable and comparable' assessment of the state of the
environment within EU member states, a number of criticisms have
been levelled at the Agency during its formative years. First, there has
been criticism regarding the source of the EEA's environmental data.
The EEA obtains its data from member states via their respective
environmental ministries. It is argued that this source provides the most
reliable form of comparable information. Critics question the reliability
of these sources, however, claiming that national ministries can filter
the information that is passed to the EEA, giving an inaccurate picture
of the state of the environment. Additionally, by restricting itself to

government sources, the EEA neglects a large source of independent analysts and groups who are not part of the national governments' network. Given this restriction Wynne and Waterton claim that:

> although the agency describes itself as a 'distributed' network, in fact its most active parts consist of a relatively restricted network, composed largely of 'official' bodies and spokespersons, in contrast to the variety of actors and institutions involved in environmental protection across Europe (Wynne and Waterton 1998: 123)

This reliance upon government sources therefore raises the question of how objective the information provided by the EEA actually is. It is argued that while incorporating information from a broader range of sources may lead to problems of comparability and accuracy, it would undoubtedly improve the perception of the EEA as an 'independent' and 'objective' environmental assessor.

The second field of criticism regarding the EEA concerns the extent of its remit and the future role which the Agency might seek to play. At present the primary focus for the EEA's activities centres around information collation for the EU. While this is an important process, many feel that the Agency would prove a more effective organization if its status was expanded to provide it with an enforcing role also. At present the EEA lacks the powers to act as an inspectorate or as an enforcer of EU environmental policy. Hence, while it is able to identify cases where member states have not met EU regulations and standards, it lacks the powers to do anything about it. Again this weakens the supposed 'objective' and independent status of the Agency. In addition it loses the support of those environmental movements who hope to see the EEA as an additional channel through which they can highlight the non-compliance of member states to EU environmental policy.

While the EEA has the potential to become a significant actor within the EU environmental policy field, the nature of the Agency's role and responsibilities means that at present it is unable to fully develop this potential. In particular, the problems highlighted above appear to place question marks over the exact role which the EEA should seek to pursue. While its proponents point to the broad array of comparable EU environmental data collated by the EEA and its significance in assessing the effectiveness of EU environmental policy, its critics identify it as a 'watchdog with no teeth', lacking any formal power to enforce the policies which it is assessing. Similarly, its reliance on government sources for data arguably restricts its claims to being objective and independent.

There is plenty of potential for the EEA to become a significant actor within the environmental policy field, however, given a broader remit within which to operate. Wynne and Waterton suggest that:

> the EEA could avoid a marginalised and ineffective role if it were allowed by its member state controllers to make its own effective partnerships with relevant providers, critics, validators, users and sources outside official government and [EU] channels—not at the expense of the latter, but on the contrary, to their ultimate benefit (Wynne and Waterton 1998: 136).

In adopting a broader role the EEA could therefore become an information source and dissemination centre for accurate and reliable comparable data on environmental standards across the EU, for not only EU institutions and member states but also broader environmental actors. It would also represent a more significant lobby focus than at present.

Raising the Environmental Standard? Assessing the Impact of Environmental Pressure

It must be reiterated that the process of lobbying surrounding environmental policy development is a far more fluid and complex process than the parameters of this chapter allow for discussion. That said, while the picture painted above may not be fully comprehensive in its coverage of all lobbying and protest activities, it does highlight the continued expansion of interest regarding the creation of an effective and influential green voice within the EU.

Overall, it would appear that the environmental actors have been very effective in placing environmental issues onto the EU policy agenda. While they may not always have gained direct access to the decision-making process and shaped environmental policies to the extent that they would have liked, both the movements and the parties have proven to be influential voices, highlighting the importance of green issues to both the general public and, subsequently, EU policy makers. As Bomberg suggests, they have 'considerable potential to act as the mouthpiece of an expanding grassroots movement, and as the agent for promoting new ideas for actual policy' (Bomberg 1998: 127). This potential is also enhanced by what appears a relatively open environment surrounding the newly emerging environmental policy networks and communities at EU level. Less success is apparent, however, when one considers the ability of the environmental actors to be part of the actual decision-making process. At this stage they appear relatively isolated.

This isolation from the policy-making arena can in part be attributed to a lack of resources. Green groups are still relatively small and poorly funded in comparison to other lobby groups and interests active within the EU; they thus have to spread their resources thinly across a broad and far-ranging set of institutions and European decision-making bodies. While some sectors with an environmental commitment may be keen to discuss and cooperate, the same is not necessarily true for all aspects of the EU. In many cases environmental protection issues must challenge the interests of very strong lobby sectors and networks. Under these conditions environmental actors have found it increasingly difficult to gain a voice. That said, the greens have managed to maintain some influence by effectively utilizing the small set of resources at their disposal. In particular, 'persistence, information, representational legitimacy and a reputation as the public's environmental watchdog' (Bomberg 1998: 128). These can, and have, proven effective weapons in influencing the development of environmental policy at EU level.

The issue of resources only represents one part of the picture, however. The relative weakness of the environmental lobby is also part of a broader failure to coordinate between national and European movements and also between environmental movements and green parties. Undoubtedly, the broad and heterogeneous nature of the environmental movement in Europe, while being a key aspect of its distinctiveness, is also an important factor in the difficulties that have been experienced in providing a coordinated and coherent green voice. Both the parties and the movements generate a large level of public support, but appear reluctant to develop close links and supporting roles, for both ideological and strategic reasons. Greater coordination, however, would possibly allow for a more effective campaign on key issues. In particular, it would enhance the campaigning skills of both forces, combining the publicity and pressure work conducted by the European green parties in and around the EP, with the lobbying capabilities and links to the Commission cultivated by the environmental movements. At present, however, green actors are only largely visible during certain parts of the policy-making process. Grant identifies two phases during which influence is currently possible:

> At the beginning of the process, when policy responses have not become crystallised, environmental think-tanks and public policy institutes may be able to influence the policy agenda … At the end of the policy process, when implementation of Community directives is undertaken by the member states, they may be able to highlight any backsliding. Through performing a whistle blowing role, they can alert the Commission, which has limited monitoring resources of its own, to any shortcomings in policy implementation (Grant 1993: 14).

Grant's assessment would at present appear to be an accurate one. The environmental lobby is clearly most visible in the initial stages and in the enforcement of policy. There is little to suggest, however, that they are able to truly play an effective role in shaping the nature of the environmental policies which are emerging from the EU. Long suggests that this failure may result in 'better resourced, and often more focused, single issue interest groups taking ever bolder positions and arguing for a halt, or even a roll-back, in environmental legislation and policy at the European level' (Long 1998: 118). With the continuing expansion of environmental issues across EU institutions and policy fields the environmental lobby clearly needs to seek a greater role and address some of its current weaknesses.

5 |

Creating a 'Sustainable' Union: The Fifth Environmental Action Plan and Sustainable Development

The development of the environmental action programmes provides a useful case study in the progression of EU environmental policy. It also allows a judgment to be made of whether the EU's commitment to sustainable development is anything more than merely rhetorical. The main purpose of the EAPs is to lay down basic principles of environmental policy and thereby to act as a framework within which specific legislation will be enacted. They also assert current priorities and commitments and plan future action. The first action programme, which emerged as a result of the Paris Summit in 1972, represents the beginnings of a coherent environmental policy within the EU, as it set down the basic principles of EC environmental policy. This first programme, covering the period 1973–76, clearly reflects much of the environmental thinking of the period, focusing mainly on pollution control and general remedial measures. It also noted the need to integrate the environment into other policy areas and the decision-making processes at both national and Community level. Its aim, to 'improve the setting and quality of life, and the surroundings and living conditions of the peoples of the Community', was not related to environmental protection *per se*, which was entirely in keeping with the thinking of the Community at the time. It is clear, therefore, that while the first EAP is part of the move away from 'incidental measures' towards a responsive EC environmental policy, it is occurring within Dryzek's 'environmental problem solving' discourse.

The first EAP also reflected the fact that the EU did not have legal competence in the field of environmental protection at this time. As a result, the programmes are not seen as being legally binding upon the member states; rather they are viewed as political declarations, which provide a policy framework for EC action. The fact that they were political declarations meant that they had to be agreed in the Council of Ministers by consensus. As Wilkinson argues, the Council of Ministers usually approved the general approach of the EAP but does not commit itself to every point, again a result of the non-binding nature of the programmes (Wilkinson 1997: 169). Despite this, the Commission was able to exploit a clause in the first EAP to embark upon a rolling process of modification and reform of the underlining principles of policy (Jordan 1999a: 10). The second programme (1977–81) focused, therefore, upon similar measures of pollution control rather than prevention.

The third and fourth action programmes, while keeping to the general policy framework outlined above, tried to reflect the growing concern over environmental issues. The most important element of the third EAP (1982–86) was the move away from specific remedial measures to a clearer policy line and an increased emphasis upon integration into other relevant policy sectors. The fourth EAP, covering the period 1987–92, listed specific actions for various sectors and allowed for the possible use of economic instruments, like taxes and licences, for the first time (Wurzel 1993: 180). The fourth EAP also led to the setting up of the EEA. Both programmes emphasized more preventative measures and made more stringent attempts to integrate environmental protection into other policy areas. This was an important development, as it made more explicit the acceptance, found in the first EAP, that in order to solve environmental problems, it is essential that the environment be integrated into other policy areas (Bomberg 1998: 35). Both of these EAPs were heavily influenced by the ideology of ecological modernization, which argues that environmental protection is not in competition with, but rather an essential precondition for, growth and development (Weale and Williams 1993: 47).

To provide bureaucratic support for the EAP, the Environment and Consumer Protection Service (ECPS) was established in 1972 as an arm of the Industry Directorate. The fact that it was part of this DG is significant, as it shows once again that the environment was treated as an economic externality that could hinder the development of the internal market. Also significant was the fact that the ECPS had a small staff of just 15 to provide this bureaucratic support. Not only was this unit under-resourced, but it had to cope with an attitude in other DGs which saw the environment as 'at best voguish and at worst politically irrelevant' (Jordan 1999a: 5). By 1981, however, the ECPS had grown to become a Directorate General responsible for Environment, Nuclear Safety and Civil Protection. DG status also gave the environment a Commissioner, who in theory could initiate policy and fight interdepartmental battles. The creation of DG Environment can be seen as an important step forward in the EU's dealings with the environment as it provides an institutional 'sponsor'. The SEA in 1987 protected the status of DG Environment and gave it explicit responsibility for the new Community competence of environmental protection.

The most important principles of the EAPs, later introduced into the Treaties via the SEA, are the 'prevention principle' and the 'polluter-pays principle'. The EAPs also wanted to see the incorporation of environmental concerns at the earliest possible stage in the decision-making process, while accepting that subsidiarity was important. They responded to one of the major environmental concerns of transnational pollution by stating that activities in member states should not take place at the expense of environmental deterioration in other member states. The EAPs argue that exploitation of nature and natural resources should be avoided and that policy decisions must take account of the interests of developing countries, recognizing the international dimension of environmental issues. Finally, they accept that it was important to raise public awareness about environmental problems (Connelly and Smith 1999: 228).

There were a number of problems associated with the EAPs' attempts to integrate environmental issues into all aspects of EU decision-making. Their main weakness was that they were guides to action and as such not legally binding. Therefore, the aim of integrating the environment into other policy areas was not legally binding, meaning that the principle was rarely translated into action (Lenschow 1999: 92). There was also the problem associated with the bureaucratic support for the environment. Having a separate DG for the environment tends to identify the environment as a separate policy area. Much like gender, however, environmental problems cut across a number of policy sectors, in this case trade, agriculture, industry, taxation, energy, transport, aid and scientific research. This fact can often bring DG Environment into conflict with other DGs, illustrating the problems of intersectoral policy coordination within the EU. For example, trade and environmental priorities can conflict, as in the case of leghold traps, which pitted DG Environment against DG External Relations (previously

DGI). A 1991 Regulation set out to ban the import of furs from countries that still used these leghold traps. DG External Relations argued against the Regulation, which had been agreed by the Environment Council, citing adverse trade implications. In the end, DG External Relations appeared to have got its way when in 1997 a watered-down proposal was presented to, and accepted by, the Council (Bretherton and Vogler 1999: 82).

A further problem for DG Environment is that the impression of it as a 'weak and peripheral player' has changed little (Jordan 1999b: 74). It is still regarded as a junior player and indeed its location, on the outskirts of Brussels, offers an insight into the way it is viewed by other parts of the Commission (Peterson and Bomberg 1999: 192). The remit of DG Environment is wide, but it has few day-to-day responsibilities for directly applying existing EU environmental policy as this task usually lies with either national or regional governments (Butt Philip 1998: 266). Its small budget and small staff, many of whom are on secondment from other EU institutions, private organizations and foundations, also weaken it. For example, in 1996–97 DG Environment had a workforce of 490 out of a total Commission staff of around 12,000.

EAP Legislation

The main weaknesses of the first four EAPs were that they were largely prescriptive and tended to impose legislation from the centre. These so-called 'command-and-control' directives and regulations tended to reflect the legislative traditions of the leader countries. They are characterized by direct regulation from the centre, which prescribe uniform environmental standards and, in some cases, the methods required to meet these standards (Golub 1998: 1). By 1998, the EU had adopted over 200 pieces of secondary legislation involving environmental protection, over 90% in the form of directives[1] (Cichowski 1998: 390). This is unsurprising as directives allow member states to choose the most appropriate method of implementation and as a result are seen as a flexible way of introducing legislation that reflects different national traditions. The other main advantage of these 'command-and-control' measures was the fact that the costs of compliance fell largely on national and local government, as well as individual economic actors, rather than on the relatively small Community budget (Butt Philip

---

1. Table 5.1 illustrates the main types of EU legislation.

1998: 264). The fact that the costs of environmental legislation are not borne by DG Environment can help to explain the levels of non-compliance with EU environmental legislation. Non-compliance is an important and often overlooked area of study, as implementation is at the 'sharp end' of the policy process (Jordan 1999b: 69). The current Environment Commissioner, Wallström, who noted that the environmental policy regulatory framework is broadly speaking in place, takes up this point that implementing existing legislation is a priority. 'If the member states were to fully apply our existing standards and rules, much would be gained already' (European Policy Centre website, accessed 13 September 2000).

Table 5.1. The Framework for EU Legislation

Type of legislation	Impact of legislation
Regulations	Binding in their entirety and directly applicable in all member states. Mostly technical and specific and apply to CAP.
Directives	Binding in the result to be achieved, but left to national authorities to decide the method to achieve this result. Must be transposed into national law.
Decisions	Binding in their entirety but addressed to a specific party or member state, i.e. competition policy ruling, exemptions to EU rules etc.
Opinions or Recommendations	Issued by Council, Commission or EP. Have no binding force but the ECJ sometimes refers to them in its decisions, making their status legally ambiguous

Source: Adapted from Peterson and Bomberg 1999.

The fact that responsibility for the implementation of legislation is shared between the Commission and the member states impacts upon how effectively environmental policy is implemented. Each member state has its own individual administrative and legal structures, along with different political cultures, all of which play a role when examining implementation (Butt Philip 1998: 266). These problems are compounded by the fact that it is the responsibility of member states to inform the Commission of compliance, a procedure that in the past was neither rigorously nor uniformly followed (Jordan 1999b: 74-75). The

Commission has the power to ensure that legislation is being enforced and can take the member state to the ECJ. However, the fact that the Commission relies upon the member states themselves to provide this information makes the situation unsatisfactory. The information on non-compliance appears to reflect the leader–laggard dimension, with Denmark at the bottom and Spain at the top. Yet, there is also strong evidence to show that compliance among laggard countries is not far off those of the leader countries and so the picture is quite complicated (see Borzel 2000). For example, two other leaders, Germany and the Netherlands, do not fare so well in the implementation table. They may fail to comply because they believe that their own national legislation conforms with the laws, when it does not (Collins and Earnshaw 1993: 220), or even that they see their legislation as more effective than EU directives (Borzel 2000). There is also the problem that some states with good general records of implementation are punished because they inform the Commission of their non-compliance, while those member states with poor implementation records are rewarded for 'forgetting' to inform the Commission.

The strength or weakness of environmental pressure groups within a member state can have a major role to play in the monitoring of implementation. The growing public awareness of the environment during the 1980s led to a significant increase in the number of complaints received by DG Environment, from nine in 1984 to over 460 in 1989 (Jordan 1999b: 76). The role that pressure groups are able to play has been made easier by the gradual development of a culture of openness within the EU, with an official recognition of the rights of individuals to request environmental information on the member states. Pressure groups also act as the Commission's 'eyes and ears' on the ground highlighting cases of non-compliance and providing the DG Environment with the political legitimacy to act. Environmental movements in the UK have been especially active in this area, including setting up their own monitoring systems. The result was that by 1990, one-third of all complaints received by the Commission originated from Britain (Connelly and Smith 1999: 224). The problem with this public demand-led approach is that the focus may only fall upon the most politically contentious issues which are 'not necessarily the most serious or the most urgent cases' (in Jordan 1999b: 81). The reliance of DG Environment upon these groups to provide details of non-compliance, also means that those countries with the weakest environmental pressure groups may be able to avoid detection. It could also be argued that it is these countries that need strong EU environmental legislation to protect the environment the most. The rise in complaints from pressure groups also adds to the problems faced by DG Environment, as it does not have the staff to deal with all cases of possible non-compliance. There is only one Desk Officer in the enforcement unit assigned to deal with compliance in each member state. Delays of up to six years between complaint and ruling are not uncommon, and could get worse if the size of DG Environment is not increased.

To improve compliance the Commission could try to issue more regulations than directives. In the past, member states have tended to view directives as 'commitments of policy intention' rather than legal obligations. Although this view has changed over recent years, it can be seen that the flexibility of directives is their major weakness. Regulations would remove this flexibility, but would they alter compliance? Member states have a legal obligation to implement all types of EU directives; therefore, many green pressure groups would argue that to improve compliance, there must be an independent monitor of implementation. As can be seen, DG Environment is too small to be able to monitor compliance efficiently and it is unlikely that the member states would countenance an increase in its powers, budget or personnel. There could also be the potential for a conflict of interest between its role as legislative proposer and enforcer. The EP argued that the EEA should have the right of inspection and of assessing compliance with legislation, but the member states vetoed this proposal for three main reasons. First, it was viewed as an information gatherer; secondly, adding the inspectorate role from the beginning would have added too much of a burden upon the EEA. Finally, there was also the possibility of its role as a mediator conflicting with the enforcer role (Connelly and Smith 1999: 243). There thus remains the possibility of the EEA becoming a fully-fledged inspectorate in the future or even an 'inspectorate of the inspectorates', monitoring the work of national inspectorates. This is more likely as there have been growing calls for minimum criteria for environmental inspections to be established in the member states to improve the enforcement of EU environmental law. Whatever happens will require the backing of the member states, which may not wish to have an independent body paying too close attention to its implementation of costly EU directives.

The Fifth Environmental Action Programme: Towards Sustainability

All the factors highlighted above have obviously hindered the development of the EU measures to tackle environmental pollution. Despite that, EAPs have become a regular feature of the EU's environmental policy and 'opened a field for Community action not originally provided for in the treaties' (Hildebrand 1993: 20). Skilful exploitation of a clause in the first EAP by the Commission had produced four action programmes of steadily increasing complexity and scope, each setting more ambitious goals and standards (Jordan 1999a: 10). This once again illustrates the incremental nature of EU policy making, as well as providing the framework for the fifth EAP (Baker 1997: 94). Despite these programmes, environmental degradation continued largely unabated. During the period of the previous EAPs, there had been a 'slow but relentless deterioration ... of the environment' (Butt Philip 1998: 253). The main problems were the rise in carbon dioxide (CO_2) emissions from fossil fuels, nitrous oxide emissions per head, and the quantity of municipal waste. The fifth EAP noted that a 20% increase in CO_2 emissions was likely to occur between 1987 and 2010 if there was no change in the current energy demand growth rates (CEC 1992: 23). Clearly, previous EU environmental policy was not working, especially in terms of integrating environment into other policy areas, and the fifth EAP was the beginning of a response to this failing. The other main influence was the Rio Earth Summit, which many saw as the beginning of a new ecological era. The fifth EAP was prepared just before the summit and shares most of the strategic objectives and principles agreed for Agenda 21 at the UN Conference on Environment and Development in Rio de Janeiro, 1992. The fifth EAP differed in its *exclusive* focus on the environment, however, ignoring the broader social dimensions of sustainable development (Wilkinson 1997: 158). That said, the fifth EAP represented the main vehicle for the implementation of Agenda 21 in the EU.

The legal confusion associated with the first four EAPs appeared to be found in the fifth EAP too. Wilkinson argued that the fifth EAP was not binding on EU member states or in practice on individual DGs in the Commission (Wilkinson 1997: 153). This interpretation was based upon the fact that the Council approved only the 'general approach and strategy of the programme' and not its detailed targets and timetables

(Wilkinson 1997: 159). This approval was given in the form of a non-binding resolution. The situation post-Amsterdam is a little different. Article 175(3) states that general action programmes set out priority objectives to be attained and that the Council using QMV shall adopt the measures necessary for the implementation of these programmes. According to Connelly and Smith, this article gave a new legal status to the general action programmes on the environment, implying that in the future they would be legally binding, and that, in particular, the fifth EAP would be interpreted in a stricter form than its formal status suggests (Connelly and Smith 1999: 240).

'Towards Sustainability', was said to constitute a positive break with the approach chosen in all preceding EAPs. It recognized that environmental protection was fundamental to the development of the EU, a break with the thinking expressed in the first EAP. The fifth EAP identified the purpose of environmental policy as follows:

> to initiate changes in the current trends and practices which are detrimental to the environment, so as to provide optimal conditions for socio-economic well-being and growth for the present and future generations (CEC 1992).

The mention of future generations showed that the fifth EAP accepted the concept of intergenerational justice, which suggests that each generation must be fair to the next. To achieve this justice, it attempted to incorporate sustainable development into all EC actions, policies and laws. Yet, as has been shown, this commitment to sustainable development in the fifth EAP was at odds with the commitment contained in the Treaties, until this was resolved at Amsterdam.

The Fifth EAP: Away from Command and Control

One main aspect of the fifth EAP's break with the past, was that it sought to supplement the 'command-and-control' directives and regulations, which were the main instruments in all previous EAPs, with more proactive policy instruments. The fifth EAP broadened the range of environmental policy instruments to include consideration of taxes and subsidies, voluntary agreements, as well as education. These new instruments were intended to provide the efficiency and positive incentives which command and control lack, without increasing the regulatory burden upon industry (Golub 1998: 5). 'Command-and-control' measures have been criticized for being economically inefficient, environmentally ineffective and democratically illegitimate. The imposition of uniform standards is seen to be economically inefficient as it does not take into account the variable pollution abatement costs facing individual firms or the local environmental situation. The result tends to be that some firms are forced to over-regulate, while others are able to meet targets which do not actually improve the environment. Hence the criticism of environmental ineffectiveness (Golub 1998: 3-4). Finally, they are seen to lack democratic legitimacy, because the public and environmental groups lack the expertise and resources to play an active role, while polluters have an incentive to 'capture' regulators to shape or block policies in accordance with their own economic self-interest (Golub 1998: 4-5).

The fifth EAP argued that long-term sustainability was important, not just for the 1993–2000 period. As a result, it reiterated the need for the environment to be fully integrated into all EU policy areas. To shift the emphasis from the 'top-down' approach reliant upon Community legislation to a 'bottom-up' approach involving all stakeholders, the fifth EAP introduced the concept of 'shared responsibility' which was intended to involve agents at global, EC, national, regional, local and also personal levels. This reflected the concerns of Agenda 21 and the 'grass-roots democracy' approach favoured by many green parties and movements. It can also be seen as an attempt to correct the democratic imbalance found in command-and-control. This bottom-up approach was also evident in the issue of implementation. In contrast to the third EAP which dealt with implementation in just three lines, the fifth EAP contained a number of proposals to strengthen consultation via the creation of a number of strategic groups linking national inspectorates and interest groups, increased national reporting and enhanced auditing (Jordan 1999b: 73, 84). All these measures were intended to improve the implementation records of member states by ensuring that legislation reflected their concerns rather than being a top-down imposition.

The main sections of the fifth EAP dealt with objectives, policies and implementation programmes for the environment for 1993–2000. It focused upon the main environmental issues confronting the EU, such as climate change, acidification and air pollution. The most radical departure from previous EAPs, however, was the focus on the source of pollution not the receptor. The fifth EAP therefore tried to offer an integrated policy for the main economic sectors that can damage environment, such as industry, transport, or energy, rather than focus on the various environmental elements, such as air, water or soil. For each sector, it set targets, the policy instruments to be used in order to reach these targets, the time frame of action, and the most significant responsible actors. These included the public and private sectors, as well as the EU, national governments and local authorities (Lenschow 1999: 93). This final element reflected a view of shared responsibility, where all stakeholders need to do their bit for the environment by changing patterns of consumption and production, implying a less state-centric approach to environmental policy (Collier 1997: 4). The importance of decentralization was shown by the fact that around 40% of the fifth EAP was the implementation responsibility of local government (Connelly and Smith 1999: 238). Finally, the role of the EU as a global environmental actor was acknowledged, with the acceptance of international cooperation within the framework of Agenda 21 and the fifth EAP.

Assessing the Impact of the Fifth EAP

An evaluation of the success of integrating environmental considerations into other policy areas is crucial to any assessment of the fifth EAP, as the Commission saw integration as a prerequisite for sustainable development (Wilkinson 1997: 153). This model of sectoral integration is heavily based upon the Dutch National Environmental Policy Plan of 1989 (Weale 1996: 600). It was pushed onto the EU agenda by the Dutch government, once again showing the ability of leader states to set the direction of EU policy (Liberatore 1997: 111). The programme set policy objectives along the line of themes and priority target groups in the five main sectors identified by the fifth EAP as crucial to its success: industry, transport, energy, agriculture and forestry, and tourism. In examining the proposals for each sector, it will be possible to judge whether they met their targets, which also permits examination of the impact of the programme as a whole.

Industry
Industry was identified in the fifth EAP not only as part of the problem, but also as part of the solution. It also recognized that manufacturing companies and their environmental problems are so diverse that it did not seek to set quantitative targets. It attempted to integrate the environment into companies' plans and actions via Environmental Manage-

ment and Audit schemes. It gave recognition to 'good examples', such as plants that planned to reduce emissions. The aim here was to reward rather than punish. The theme of shared responsibility was clear in this sector as one major aim was eco-labelling, allowing consumers to make informed purchases, although a regulation which encouraged the use of eco-labels has not been widely applied. A notable exception has been the German 'Blue Swan' mark, although with Germany a clear leader state, it is perhaps unsurprising that they have implemented this regulation in full (Sbragia 2000: 312). There is also a question mark hanging over eco-labels as to whether they are protectionist, highlighting once again the clash between environmental protection and measures to complete the single market.

The four key objectives for the industry sector included sustainability of resources, prevention of pollution, waste management, and the establishment of generic auxiliary mechanisms. The Progress Report issued in 1996 to assess the impact of the action programme, argued that change in this sector is critical to the achievement of sustainable development. It stated that, despite the then recession, encouraging progress had been made towards achieving the aims (CEC 1996: 25). In part, this progress was related to the fact that legislation in this area existed long before the fifth EAP, but also many of the larger manufacturing companies saw the cost advantages in shifting to greener production methods. Commissioner Wallström cites the example of Rank Xerox that set itself the goal of zero waste. By introducing recycling in all its manufacturing sites and recovering and re-using old copiers, the company has enjoyed cost savings, a reduction in unit prices for customers and a big reduction in waste sent to landfill (European Policy Centre website, accessed 13 September 2000). They noted, however, that within small and medium-sized enterprises (SMEs) progress had been relatively slow, with increased costs the major concern, resulting in provision within the Structural Funds of 1994–99 for environmental improvements within SMEs.

Transport
The transport sector is a major contributor to the problem of pollution, especially air and noise. The fifth EAP Progress Report estimated that about 60% of carbon monoxide emissions, more than 50% of nitrous oxide and 80% of noise pollution come from transport (CEC 1996: 36). The report also predicted that increased use of transport would result in

a significant increase in these pollutants. This is another sector where it is possible to observe the 'polluting face' of the EU. For example, the promotion of Trans-European Networks are predicted to increase CO_2 emissions in the transport sector by up to 18% (see Lucas 2001). Also, measures to liberalize the airline industry have had a negative environmental impact, witnessed by the recent growth in low-cost airlines and the related increase in flights. Despite these criticisms, the Commission promoted a number of measures to try and reduce the environmental impact of this sector, including encouraging companies to shift to 'greener' fuel, subsidies to shift freight from road to rail/sea and a directive on the charging of transport infrastructure costs to lorries. The principle for shared responsibility in this sector was reflected in measures to reduce car use and encourage the use of public transport. For example, European Car Free day on 22 September 2000 encouraged people to use other forms of transport, with differing degrees of success (*Environment for Europeans* October 2000: 16). In general, these programmes have had the impact of reducing traditional pollutants, such as lead, and thus improving the quality of air in Europe.

Many green groups argue, however, that unless the cost of car use accurately reflects the environmental damage it causes, these types of measures will achieve little, although the Progress Report claimed some success in internalizing the external costs of transport. The most efficient way to achieve this would be via the use of taxes, but this aspect has yet to really take off at the EU level. Green groups also highlight that larger problems exist, such as the development of out-of-town shopping centres and the development of 'just-in-time deliveries' to supermarkets, which allow them to save on storage space, but increase the number of deliveries and force people to use their cars. In 1996, the Progress Report suggested that while traditional pollutants from transport were decreasing, traffic growth was the major threat to the EU's CO_2 strategy. Although the evidence suggests that overall the EU remains on track to meet its Kyoto target, a report in November 2000 highlighted the fact that every member state with the exception of Luxembourg was experiencing increases in greenhouse emissions from the transport sector, the fastest growing emissions source. This increase meant that current projections suggest that the strategy for this sector will fail to meet its target (*Environment for Europeans* November 2000: 6).

Energy

Like transport, the energy sector is a major source of the CO_2 emissions that contribute to global climate change. This part of the fifth EAP was designed to assist the EU achieve its UN Climate Change Convention commitment of stabilizing CO_2 emissions by 2000 at 1990 levels and by reducing them to 8% below the 1990 level by 2008–12. It uses a number of programmes to help it achieve this target. For example, SAVE I and II had the aim of stabilizing CO_2 emissions and achieving improvements in energy efficiency, while ALTENER encouraged the promotion of renewable energy sources. The latest report from the EEA in November 2000 appeared to show that the EU was on track to meet the first of these targets, although it also highlighted that these results could be related to one-off emission reductions in Germany and the UK (*Environment for Europeans* November 2000: 6).

The problem is that energy policy has a direct impact upon environmental measures and in this crucial policy sector the EU only has weak powers. Although it has shared responsibility for energy policy, the instruments for energy policy are not integrated within the treaties (Barnes and Barnes 1999: 234). The proposed liberalization and deregulation of domestic energy markets compound this situation. The main activity for the Commission as noted in the Progress Report, has been to support energy conservation and renewable energy measures. Encouraging energy conservation, especially among consumers, formed part of the shared responsibility strategy of the fifth EAP. A good example of measures to support renewable energy was a £4 million plan to investigate the potential for use of North Sea winds to power turbines, a scheme partly funded by the European Commission (*The Guardian* 3 February 2000). The critique from green NGOs and MEPs is that failure to use the full range of economic instruments, especially taxation, is likely to prevent the EU achieving its targets in this area (Lucas 2001). There is also the view that research rather than regulation is important, reflecting one again the problem-solving discourse where issues like global warming are treated as problems to be solved by new technology. DG Environment's focus upon the economic costs of environmental pollution is again highlighted in this sector. The DG stressed the fact that business can reduce costs by reducing energy bills, giving the example from the hotel industry where hotels now only wash towels that are actually dirty, helping reduce costs by decreasing the amount of laundry they have to do.

Agriculture and Forestry

The fifth EAP argued that there is a growing need to reconcile agricultural policy and the environment (CEC 1996: 45). The CAP's focus on production has led to many unacceptable environmental consequences, such as over-use of pesticides, the reduction of water resources and the removal of hedgerows. One of the main aims in this sector was to fully incorporate environmental considerations into the CAP. The main initiatives included the possibility of transferring set-aside obligations to environmentally sensitive areas, the assessment of the environmental impact of measures financed under agricultural funds, agri-environmental measures, and the exchange of good practice. The Progress Report argued that the 1992 reform of the CAP did little to systematically integrate environmental concerns (CEC 1996: 45). It argued that more needed to be done in the area of water quality. It also called for reduced reliance upon market price support to encourage more sustainable production (CEC 1996: 53). By 1996, the Progress Report was claiming success in incorporating environmental elements into future reforms of the CAP, including the reduction of price support. It is claimed, however, that some of these successes actually owe more to exogenous factors than the fifth EAP. For example, Wilkinson claimed that CAP reform was more a reflection of a coincidence of interests between the farming community and environmentalists rather than at the instigation of the fifth EAP (Wilkinson 1997: 164). Despite these criticisms, the inclusion of a measure to increase the 'greening' of the CAP in the Commission's Agenda 2000 programme can be identified as an integration success, although more needs to be done (Lenschow 1999: 103).

Tourism

Although the EU treaties do not provide the EU with the explicit competence to act in the area of tourism, they do acknowledge that EU actions should include measures in the field of tourism in order to accomplish the other tasks that are specifically assigned to the Union (CEC 1996: 57). To achieve sustainable tourism clearly involves measures from other target sectors, most obviously transport. Although data on the impact of tourism on the environment is sketchy, DG Environment identified the quality of water and land use as areas of concern. They also wished to try and reconcile tourism and development. One interesting aspect of tourism is that, like transport, it is a sector in which individuals can play a significant role, highlighting the application of shared responsibility and subsidiarity. Information is also crucial if consumers are to make informed choices. A good example is the Blue Flag Directive which states that beaches that are clean for a number of years can fly a blue flag to prove their cleanliness. This not only allows people to choose which beaches they use, but it also puts pressure on 'dirty' beaches to improve to win back tourists, something that many resorts in the north-west of England have spent millions of pounds upon in the past few years. In keeping with the stakeholder approach, the Commission have made good use of Dialogue Groups and the General Consultative Forum as ways of sharing good practice and putting this shared responsibility into operation. The Progress Report highlighted some moves towards sustainable production and consumption patterns and the growth of some sustainable tourism, but noted that more use of the Structural Funds to tackle the negative aspects of tourism would be necessary, an example of the integration principle in action. Overall, progress in this sector has been hampered by the subsidiarity principle, with some governments believing that tourism is a matter for member states only (Barnes and Barnes 1999: 275).

Problems with the Fifth EAP Instruments

The use of non-regulatory instruments by the fifth EAP was identified as one of its main strengths and a real break with previous EAPs. They are said to be more flexible and responsive to the market situation. However, reliance upon these types of instruments and the concept of shared responsibility, combined with a failure to introduce an eco-tax, have led many to criticize the fifth EAP as being too weak on industry.

Voluntary Agreements
The use of voluntary agreements and self-regulation has a long tradition in two leader states, Denmark and the Netherlands (Collier and Golub 1997: 241). They offer a number of advantages to the policy maker. They tend to be preferred by the business lobby, as they do not increase regulation or cost in the same way as market-based instruments. The problem is that they only work if people are prepared to modify their behaviour. They also rely on business to reach an agreement in the first place and then self-regulate. So far, across the EU there appears to be a distinct lack of enthusiasm from business. By the end of 1998 only 12

products were covered by EU eco-labels and in many of these cases it had taken years for the criteria to be constructed. Some industries, for example cosmetics, refused to cooperate in discussions over any product because it opposed the proposed criteria for hairsprays. It therefore appeared that, despite pressure from industry for these new ways of regulation to ensure competitiveness, 'firms seem reluctant to cooperate in establishing the criteria for, and then using, eco-labelling for their products unless there is a threat of binding regulation, except in a few technically homogeneous sectors' (Sbragia 2000: 312). Environmental NGOs and the EP are therefore sceptical about the use of these new instruments. However, this may have more to do with the fact that the EP has more control over traditional EU legislation than representing any environmental critique of voluntary agreements (European Policy Centre website, accessed 13 September 2000). Despite these criticisms, some achievements have been observed, most notably the July 1998 agreement to limit the CO_2 emissions from new cars, signed despite scepticism from the EP, which wanted binding legislation (Sbragia 2000: 312). Commissioner Wallström has said that she is in favour of making more use of these types of agreements, although she stressed that they are only an option if they present advantages compared to other instruments. She also stressed that if voluntary agreements do not work, the introduction of stricter EU legislation is unavoidable (*Eur-op News* 2000). DG Environment is therefore pursuing a twin-track strategy of encouraging voluntary agreements with the veiled threat of legislation if this does not succeed.

Shared Responsibility

Shared responsibility is one of the major planks of the fifth EAP. It shifts part of the responsibility for environmental protection onto consumers and citizens. In short, it states that everyone must take responsibility for his or her actions. What is clear from our analysis is that this has been one of the most problematic areas. As Commissioner Wallström highlighted, one of the most difficult changes to achieve is the behaviour of consumers, transport users and tourists. Car use is increasing, recycling rates are minimal and international travel is increasingly commonplace. All of these have an impact on the environment. The fuel tax protests across the EU in the summer of 2000 suggested that despite opinion polls indicating green attitudes among many people, when push comes to shove, people vote with their wallets. This was also evidenced by the reluctance of many European governments to use the 'green card' to defend high petrol prices.

The counter-point to this is that policy makers have yet to engage the public in a debate about the need for changing consumption patterns. As long as the political debate revolves around who can cut taxes, deregulate the labour market and so on, there is little room for a debate about how our actions affect the planet. The 1996 Progress Report highlighted the problem of a low level of environmental awareness among European 'stakeholders', including how their own activities have an impact on the environment. DG Environment therefore stressed the importance of incorporating environmental protection considerations into citizens' daily lives. Increased education is their preferred strategy, but it is clear that, in this area, the reality lags far behind the political ideal.

Why No Eco-tax? A Reflection of the Weakness of the Fifth EAP
One of the most controversial aspects of the fifth EAP was its support for increased use of taxation to achieve its targets. The general aim of eco-taxation involves a gradual shift of taxation from 'goods' such as employment, to 'bads' such as pollution, and promises a range of benefits from increased energy efficiency to lower unemployment. Eco-taxes could be used in most of the fifth EAP sectors, but as yet have not featured in EU efforts to tackle environmental problems. This is despite eco-taxes becoming a recognized policy instrument and many experts arguing that 'eco-taxes are indispensable to tackling the problems of excessive production of waste and pollution and excessive demand for key resources' (Christie 1999: 34).

Eco-taxes offer the possibility of a more efficient way of tackling environmental problems, with some estimates suggesting that a single economic instrument, such as a tax on fuel, could replace the 117 'regulatory' directives in force in the EU relating to the environment. Despite this, progress at the EU level has been very slow (see Luckin and Lightfoot 1999). The main reason for this is the fact that unanimity is required in the Council for all issues related to taxation. Attempts to introduce QMV for environmental fiscal policy were blocked at both Amsterdam and Nice, despite consistent pressure from some of the institutions of the EU. The other reason is that taxation issues remain on the Ecofin rather than the Environment Council agenda. The result has been that all Commission proposals for an EU-wide energy/carbon tax have thus far failed (Schlegelmilch 1998: 3-8). For example, the relatively ambitious energy tax proposed by the Commission in the early 1990s was, by 1997, replaced by a far more modest proposal for harmonization of minimum rates of tax on energy products. Yet even this proposal was blocked by a number of governments, including the then right-wing administrations of France, Spain and Britain. Leader states, such as the Netherlands, have consistently championed the adoption of environmental taxes at the EU level since the early 1990s, in part to avoid the 'unacceptable competitive disadvantages' brought about by national eco-taxes (Liefferink 1997: 235). In 1998, the Dutch attempted to make the 'burden-sharing' deal, which was reached in relation to climate change policy commitments following the Kyoto Conference, conditional on the adoption of an EU-wide energy tax by 2002. Again, opposition from other member states stalled the proposal. The Dutch position was rejected by Michael Meacher on behalf of the new British Government: 'There is no conditionality, there never could be' (*Environmental Daily Service (ENDS)* 17 June 1998).

Despite these setbacks, a number of member states have introduced national schemes and the enthusiasm of institutions like the EEA and the EP for the coordinated use of European environmental taxes has not been blunted by the repeated failures to make progress (Schlegelmilch 1998). The EP's Olsson Report of July 1998 once again raised the issue of an eco-tax, stressing the job-creating potential of an ecological tax reform: the so-called 'double dividend' (Schlegelmilch 1998: 7). The influence of the EP is limited by the fact that for fiscal matters, it only has the right of consultation. Even the leader countries have also been unable to project 'green' policies on to the EU in this area. The new German government, however, having introduced a national eco-tax (see Lightfoot and Luckin: 2000), expressed a desire to make progress on this issue at the European level but the results of the German presidency of the EU during the first six months of 1999 were disappointing. The German environment minister, Jürgen Trittin, indicated that the government would pursue the adoption of higher energy taxes to finance lower taxes on employment within the EU and the termination of the international tax exemption for aviation fuel during its presidency. Despite this, neither proposal was acted upon. One illustration of problems relating to eco-taxation can be seen by the variety of positions adopted by the new Labour Government in the UK. Prior to the Amsterdam Summit, they explicitly ruled out any extension of

QMV in environmental policy to fiscal matters (Labour Party 1995: 5). Then in an apparent softening of this position, on the eve of the 1999 European Elections Blair and Schröder issued a joint statement that included reference to the rebalancing of the taxation burden to environmental 'bads'. By the time of the Nice IGC in December 2000, this attitude had changed again, with the British Government, along with six other member states, 'red-lining' taxation policy as an issue where the national veto must remain. This suggested that, once again, short-term domestic political factors appear to have taken precedence over longer-term environmental consideration. Optimists point to increased green participation in governments throughout the EU and Commissioner Wallström's support for an energy tax as the strongest incentive available to lower dependency upon fossil fuels and develop renewable energy sources, hints of eco-taxes to come.

Impact of the Fifth EAP

When reviewing the impact of the fifth EAP halfway through its course, DG Environment noted that their mood was one of 'cautious optimism'. They believed that 70% of commitments at EU level have been achieved, but that progress in the member states was more difficult to discern (CEC 1996: 10). In part this related back to the small size of the monitoring staff in the DG and their reliance upon member states and environmental NGOs for information. More worrying for the success of the fifth EAP was that DG Environment found major problems incorporating environmental considerations in each policy area. This inability to achieve a large degree of integration was related to the difficulties of working across different aspects. The problem highlighted over the issue of integration in previous EAP's appeared to haunt the fifth EAP. In the 1996 Progress Report, DG Environment argued that

> the measures so far have had limited impact ... progress has varied according to sectors, but the message of the fifth EAP has not been sufficiently integrated in operational terms within the Commission. The process depends on persuasion and influence and will take time. In the longer term, change is likely to take place through increased education, training and changes of attitude. It will require continued adequate resources and sustained commitment (CEC 1996).

Wilkinson has highlighted the main organizational ways the Commission has aimed for sectoral integration. DG Environment has an

Integration Unit, which monitors the implementation of the EAPs both in DG Environment and throughout the Commission. This unit is the main point of contact for the Integration correspondents, whose job it is to ensure that policies within their DG take proper account of the environment. In theory, this person was to be a senior official, but in practice the task is usually delegated (Wilkinson 1997: 160-61). The Commission also requires an environmental appraisal to be carried out of any Commission proposal likely to have a significant impact upon the environment. Each DG is expected to carry out an annual evaluation of its environmental performance, although DG Environment noted that

> numerous DGs, have taken initiatives and developed measures in the environment sector, but to what extent and how the environment has been taken into account, on a systematic basis, as other types of measures and policies are devised, is rarely indicated (Wilkinson 1997: 163).

The main problem for DG Environment is that it has no formal power over the other DGs. Echoing a theme illustrated above, former Commissioner Bjerregaard observed that:

> I am a bit like someone in charge of a carpark where none of the issues which are parked there under the name of the environment are really ones that I could call my own. In reality they are in fact issues which really need to be resolved elsewhere by some of my other Commission colleagues... (in Wilkinson 1997: 160).

This has been evidenced by the fact that many parts of the Commission showed a distinct lack of enthusiasm for promptly publishing those reports on implementation that are legally required of it (Haigh 1999: 111). There is also the question of money. Spending on the CAP and the Structural Funds take up the majority of the relatively small EU budget, yet projects they fund can often have damaging consequences for the environment (Lenschow 1999). As well as wishing to see a further 'greening' of the CAP and the Structural Funds, many would argue that to tackle the environmental problems within Europe today needs an increase in the amount of the EU budget spent upon environmental improvements. For example, at present the LIFE fund for environmental improvements accounts for only 0.1% of the total budget (Christie 1999: 33). To counter these problems of integrating sustainability throughout the Commission obviously requires strong political leadership. Christie (1999) proposes the radical solution that a Sustainable Development Unit should be created in the Commission President's office. This unit would be staffed by a cross-directorate team, led by an assistant to the President of Commissioner rank, who would be responsible for an overarching Sustainable Development Strategy for the EU. It would also act as a broker for issues that cut across two or more DGs' areas of responsibility, overcoming one of the major problems identified with integrating environmental issues into all areas of policy. The work of the unit should then be shadowed by an annual sustainability summit. This solution also anticipates the EP paying greater attention to environmental and social sustainability criteria, and also requiring that every new policy proposal from the Commission include a statement on its contribution to both sustainable development and the environment (Christie 1999: 29-30). As yet, none of these proposals have been acted upon within the Commission.

The issue of integration also brings with it specific challenges for DG Environment. As Haigh foresaw in 1984, the simple sounding statement concerning the need for integration represented a considerable challenge for the Environment DG. The new departure entailed in this declaration means:

> that environmental policy will cease to be a fairly self-contained activity within the Commission and the Directorate-General for the Environment will have to involve itself much more in the work of others. This may well be seen as interference by those responsible for, say, agriculture, transport and energy policy, and anyone with experience of bureaucracies know what that entails' (in Haigh 1999: 110).

Despite being written 16 years ago, Haigh's comments still reflect the situation today, although the example seems to only suggest a one-way process of influence with DG Environment involving itself in the activities of other DGs. This view has been criticized by those who view integration as a double-edged sword. At the same time as other DGs have been opened up to DG Environment, it has also become more open to other DGs. For example, Sbragia notes that many DGs have used the integration principle to make DG Environment aware of the 'real world' problems faced by industry (Sbragia 2000: 299). This may suggest that DG Environment is being taken more seriously by the other DGs and that at long last they are paying attention to what emanates from within DG Environment. There is also evidence that other DGs still view DG Environment as too 'green' and too idealistic and are welcoming the chance to restrain their younger upstart. With the increasing realization of environmental problems and a growing acceptance of the need for integration, it is likely that DG Environment will be in a much stronger position to force the pace of integration in the future. In doing so, it runs the risk of becoming a victim of its own environmental enthusiasm for the integration principle. If environmental concerns are successfully integrated into other policy areas and responsibility passes to the sectoral DGs so that, for example, measures to prevent or minimize agricultural or industrial pollution become the exclusive responsibility of the agricultural and industrial DGs, why is it necessary to have a separate environmental DG? (Wilkinson 1997: 164-65).

In 1996 the Commission adopted a draft decision aimed at improving the environment and moving towards sustainable development, based upon the conclusions of the Progress Report and the EEA's 'State of the Environment' report. This draft decision identified five priority areas in which EU action needed to be improved. They were:

- improved integration with other policy sectors;
- the use of a wider range of policy instruments;
- increased implementation and enforcement measures by improved and simplified legislation;
- raising public awareness;
- reinforcing the EU's international role.

The fact that many of these priority areas were merely restating the aims of the fifth EAP offered some idea of the problem of integration and questioned the extent of its practical ability to meet its objectives.

This proposal was sent to the EP and Council for adoption under the co-decision procedure. The EP adopted 28 amendments to the Council opinion, which the Council was unable to accept, so the issue went to conciliation. Finally, 30 months after the initial Commission proposal, a co-decision was reached. The result of their conciliation process was that the text was weakened, especially with regard to the integration of the environment into agriculture and the issue of environmental liability. The result of the Cardiff Summit, however, was that different sectoral Councils must take account of sustainable development issues in their actions, and report to future EU summits on their strategies for integration (Christie 1999: 28). At the Vienna Summit in December 1998, the Transport, Energy and Agricultural Councils reported on their initial strategies. At the same summit, three more Councils—Industry, Internal Market, and Development—were invited to submit similar reports to the next summit in Helsinki. The 'Cardiff Process' also required the Commission to strengthen its assessment of its own proposals as the 'green star' scheme had proved to be inadequate. It is clear from this discussion that for the first time the member states are taking the issue of integration more seriously.

Towards the Sixth EAP

Despite criticisms, EAPs form a crucial plank of the EU's attempts to combat environmental pollution and to move towards sustainable development. In early 2001 the Commission launched its sixth EAP. This new programme built upon a consultation launched by the Commission in November 1999 with its Global Assessment of the fifth EAP, which in turn was based upon a major report by the EEA on the state of the environment. This Global Assessment examined whether any of the objectives and priorities needed revising or updating. The fifth EAP 'radical' aim was for long-term sustainability. The Commission could therefore have just renewed the fifth EAP rather than drawing up a new programme. According to Commissioner Wallström although much of the fifth programme remained valid, the Commission wished to update the EU's political priorities and to include some new issues. Therefore the sixth EAP 'Our Future, Our Choice' is seen as an attempt to tackle those areas where the fifth EAP failed to make significant progress, plus new areas such as soil erosion and the regulation of chemicals (*Environment for Europeans* March 2001: 3).

The Global Assessment conclusions highlighted that while pollution levels were being reduced, many problems remained and unless they were rectified quickly the environment would continue to deteriorate. Its conclusions were backed up by the EEA's Second Assessment of the European Environment. Both reports highlighted the environmental problems the EU faces. They also showed that issues such as poor implementation of legislation by member states, the poor integration of the environment into other policy areas, and the failure of shared responsibility, continued to prevent the EU attaining the standards it sets for itself. There was also the perennial problem of reconciling environmental imperatives with the socioeconomic objectives of the EU. One of the main disappointments of the fifth EAP was the fact that emission reductions in one sector could be offset by increases in another, as was seen in the transport and energy sectors. The sixth EAP tries to incorporate solutions to these problems, but in most areas is limited to setting general objectives rather than quantified targets. Commissioner Wall-ström argued that 'it is important that we discuss concrete actions that will start things moving rather than spend much time in debating what the specific target figures should be' (DG Environment website, accessed 8 May 2001).

The sixth EAP highlighted four key areas where action must be taken: climate change; protecting nature and diversity; environment and health; and resources and waste management. According to the Swedish Government, which represented the Council Presidency during the first half of 2001, climate change is one of the biggest threats to sustainable development. The continuing need to reduce emissions was illustrated by an EEA Report in May 2001, which showed that a number of member states had exceeded their emission targets agreed as part of the 'burden sharing' deal agreed in Luxembourg 1998. This deal was designed to allow the EU to meet the Kyoto Protocol target of an 8% reduction in emissions over 1990 levels by 2008–12. Despite these problems, the Commission called for more far-reaching global emission cuts in the order of 40% by 2020 and cites the scientific estimate that in the longer term a 70% global greenhouse gas emission reduction as compared to 1990 will be needed. The programme pointed to the need for structural changes especially in the transport and energy sectors, called for stronger efforts in energy-efficiency and energy-saving, the establishment of an EU-wide emissions trading scheme, further research and technological development and awareness-raising with citizens so that they can contribute to reducing emissions. Commissioner Wallström stressed that 'the scientists have told us clearly that we must face up to climate change or else accept dramatic consequences. Making the Kyoto Protocol operational is not easy as everybody knows but it can really only be a first step' (DG Environment website, accessed 8 May 2001). Many NGOs are concerned that the EEA figures suggest that a number of countries, including leader states, are on course to overshoot their targets. If the EU fails once again to tackle one of the major environmental problems it faces, it will not just cause problems for its sustainability strategy. As Hans Wolters, Director of Greenpeace International, argued 'we can't wait too long anymore to do something real about climate change … or it will be too late' (European Policy Centre website, accessed 8 May 2001). Once again the lack of an EU-wide eco-tax has prompted criticism that the commitments in the sixth EAP are unlikely to be achieved.

The need to reduce intra-EU emissions must also be seen in the light of the decision taken by the new Bush administration in the USA to back out of their Kyoto commitments; a decision that confirmed the position adopted by US officials during the Hague Climate Change Summit in November 2000. During the Gothenburg Summit in June 2001, the EU leaders committed themselves to ratify the Kyoto protocol by the end of 2001, with President Bush's pledge not to block the Kyoto process providing some optimism that a deal could still be struck with the world's largest polluter. The EU's position was welcomed by various green NGOs, with Dennis Pamlin, the WWF climate change campaign coordinator, stating that the 'EU continues to lead the world on climate change' (*Financial Times* 17 June 2001). This episode high-lighted that, at least internationally, the EU has moved further onto a sustainability agenda.

While climate change is arguably the biggest global threat, the sixth EAP acknowledges the threat of losing the unique resource of nature and bio-diversity within Europe, with the biggest threats coming from unsustainable farming and fishing.

The sixth EAP argues that Europe is seeing dramatic threats to the survival of many species and their habitats. The full establishment of the Natura 2000 network and a set of sectoral bio-diversity action plans are the cornerstones of the approach to avert these threats. In addition, more attention needs to be given to protecting landscapes more gener-ally through agricultural and regional policies. The programme also announced new initiatives for protecting the marine environment and proposals to prevent industrial and mining accidents. Finally, a thematic strategy for protecting soils will open a new field of Community environmental policy.

The sixth EAP also for the first time makes an explicit link between health and the environment by calling for a holistic approach to envi-ronment and health, arguing for the implementation of the precau-tionary principle due to the impact of a poor environment on vulnerable groups, such as children and the elderly. In this area the Commissioner gave a robust defence of the position not to set targets: 'how do we set limits when our health is at risk? In statistics the "norm" is usually a male adult. But we also need to find out what limits apply to vulnerable groups, such as children and pregnant women, to avoid their being harmed' (*Environment for Europeans* March 2001: 3). 'Our future, Our Choice' stressed the need to decouple resource use from growth. As countries get richer, so their resource use increases, but their recycling does not. So while resources are being depleted, waste builds up, offering additional environmental and health problems.

To improve conditions in these four priority areas, the sixth EAP argues that it offers a strategic approach. It re-emphasizes the need to integrate environmental concerns into economic sectors and other policy areas to ensure that the environmental objective of a sustainable society is achieved. Full integration of environmental concerns into the four policy priority areas is clearly crucial for the EU to meet its objectives, as is full implementation of existing legislation, such as the Water Framework Directive and the Noise Framework Directive. To ensure implementation, the EAP focuses upon legal action via the ECJ alongside a 'name and shame' policy. The EAP once again highlighted the business opportunities offered by clean technology and eco labels. Commissioner Wallström sees this as the cornerstone of her own agenda:

> I believe that 'greening' the market is a key to sustainable development. And I know that there are many pro-active companies out there who already benefit economically from the high environmental standards they apply, and which consumers are expecting more and more (DG Environment website, accessed 8 May 2001).

This theme of working with business and consumers to achieve more environmentally friendly forms of production and consumption echoes the theme of shared responsibility found in the fifth EAP. Here, the Commission wants to have recourse to a raft of new instruments ranging from an integrated product policy, which encourages a sustainable life for products from design to disposal, and environmental liability to fiscal measures and better information for citizens. This stress on working with the market appears to be part of a developing problem-solving discourse, which clearly still exists within the EU.

The sixth EAP was initially criticized by some Green MEPs as weak and the EP's support was only achieved after Commissioner Margot Wallström accepted many of their amendments. The Green/European Free Alliance (EFA) Group claimed that improvements to the first Commission proposal were only included due to their pressure. Inger Schörling MEP, a Swedish Green Member of the Environment Committee said that 'the European Parliament succeeded in clarifying the timetable and setting out concrete measures for new action fields such as soil protection, marine environment and others, which the EU

Commission wanted to be left vague'. The fact that the European People's Party (EPP), the largest group in the Parliament, voted against the sixth EAP suggests that Parliament's amendments may have difficulty surviving the co-decision procedure with the Council of Ministers.

Also, despite the Green Group's proposals, the sixth EAP in many ways does not appear that much different from its predecessor and looks likely to face many of the same problems. NGOs see the incorporation of the environment into all other sectoral policies as crucial to its success. In this area, many believe there is still a long way to go towards changing the mentality of policymakers from thinking merely in sectoral compartments. This need to incorporate the environment fully and also to implement existing legislation fully is crucial with enlargement a very real prospect. While monitoring the implementation of EU legislation still remains in the hands of member states, however, the existing levels of implementation are unlikely to be radically improved. Finally, some of the suggested economic instruments, such as taxation and policy areas, including land use and planning, are still decided by unanimity. This means that proposals often run the risk of becoming the lowest common denominator.

The development of the sixth EAP must also be seen alongside the Commission's sustainable development strategy launched at the Gothenburg Summit in June 2001. This is seen as part of a long march towards sustainability, although there was still some debate around the proper definition of the concept. The decision on a strategy for sustainable development, seen by Swedish Prime Minister Persson as a 'huge one in European history', adds an environment dimension to the EU's existing economic and social policy objectives. The Swedish Presidency and the European Commission wished to set firm environmental targets to mirror those for economic and social policies agreed at the Lisbon Summit in 2000, but like the sixth EAP, the final strategy contained few concrete targets. Both the Swedish Presidency and the subsequent Belgium Presidency identified the Sustainability Summit in Johannesburg in 2002 as a possible starting point to signal that the EU is ready to change its unsustainable consumption and production patterns. The EU has also promised progress towards reaching the United Nations' long-standing official development aid target of 0.7% of GDP before this summit. The fact that the EU committed itself to sustainable development back in Rio in 1992 highlights the difficulties faced in creating a sustainable Union.

Ideological Critique of the EAPs

The difficulties in creating a sustainable Union, for critics of the EAPs, are based upon the fact that the 'EU is structurally incapable of catering for environmental concerns' (Lucas 2001). The organization is committed to the 'rhetoric of ecological modernisation and weak sustainability' (Connelly and Smith 1999: 239). The ideology of ecological modernization has come under fire for regarding the economic benefits of protecting the environment as an important goal in its own right (Baker 1997: 96). To many environmentalists this type of thinking is an anathema. Ecological modernization can also be viewed more positively. It is seen as a new framework for understanding the environment-economy problem. Jacobs argues that ecological modernization:

> reinterprets the environmental problem as one of economic restructuring ... a shift onto a new path of economic development in which technological advances and social changes combine to reduce, by an order of magnitude, the environmental impacts of economic activity (Jacobs 1999: 9-10).

While this definition may not go as far as some would wish, it could have an impact upon pollution levels in the EU. The fifth EAP tried to reconcile the EU's 'historic commitment to economic development with its new concern to protect the environment' (Baker *et al.* 1997: 30). The development of EU environmental policy from the Treaty of Rome onwards has seen the focus shift from one solely based upon economics to a broader based quality of life ethos. This, plus the incremental nature of EU policy making, make it unsurprising that the EU has adopted measures that reflect 'managerial as opposed to radical policy solution' (Baker 1997: 102). It could also be argued that the EU is rarely ever socially or ecologically radical due to the difficulties associated with the joint-decision trap. Whether the sixth EAP changes this perception radically is unlikely, but ecological events may force the EU's hand.

The Future of Policy Integration

The EAPs have offered an opportunity to judge the development of the EU's success in the environmental field. Its principles and policies can be seen to counter the negative application of subsidiarity by member states, as well as leading all member states towards a common environmental policy (Connelly and Smith 1999: 240). Even if not everyone would agree with the EU's definition of sustainable development, or even believe that it could achieve its own targets, the fact that it has committed itself to sustainable development is significant. It also gives a yardstick by which to judge the success or failure of future EU policies. The fifth EAP can also be seen as an important development not just for the environment but for the future of European integration as a whole. As the EEA argued:

> the long term success of the more important initiatives such as the internal market and monetary union will be dependent upon the sustainability of the policies pursued in the fields of industry, energy, transport, agriculture and regional development ... This implies the integration of environmental considerations in the formulation and implementation of economic and sectoral policies, in the decisions of public authorities, in the conduct and development of production processes and individual behaviour and choice (in Lenschow 1999: 93).

The pressure is therefore on the sixth EAP to continue the work started but also to ensure that past failures are not repeated.

6 |

Greening the Union: Environmental Progress or 'Green' Window-Dressing?

This book has examined the impact of environmental theory, pressure and policy making upon the changing nature of the EU. We have undoubtedly witnessed an expansion of green influence from within all of these dimensions, especially within the last twenty years. However, it has also become evident that while this examination highlights a far greater emphasis upon environmental issues within the contemporary EU, there is still some way to go before one can truly claim that it has developed into the proactive environmental guardian that it has the potential to be.

The aim of this final chapter, therefore, is to provide an assessment of the progress that has been made by the EU within the environmental sphere. To establish a clear overview of the progression that the EU has made in this field, however, requires an assessment of these developments and changes across three different levels, which reflect the standpoints adopted and developed in this book. First, a very practical approach to the issue, assessing whether or not environmental policy emerging at the EU level has made any real impact on the state of the environment. Quite simply, does the rhetoric of environmental policy making translate into the realities of practical change? Is there any evidence from the developments outlined above, to suggest that the state of the natural world has been improved through the actions of the EU and its member states? Similarly, is it accurate to claim that EU environmental policy has altered the actions of the member states with regard to the environment?

Secondly, one must address concerns about the more indirect impact of the emerging development of an environmental discourse within the EU. Chapter 2 highlighted the diverse ways in which the environmental issue was approached and assessed, and noted that although there has been relative agreement as to the problems, there has been much more diversity in approaches towards addressing the problems and providing solutions. In particular, Dryzek's categorization highlighted the distinctions between different degrees of environmental commitment. By drawing upon these ideas again here, one can assess whether or not the discourse towards environmental issues within the EU has altered. Has the manner in which the EU addresses environmental problems changed as environmental policy has evolved? In particular, is there any evidence, from the pattern of policy development outlined within this book, which suggests a growing influence for the environmental discourse espoused within green political theory and green pressure groups upon both the approach to, and the framework for, EU environmental policy?

Finally, the discussion builds upon these previous levels and involves a more predictive assessment regarding the possible future for environmental policy, and more broadly, green politics within the EU. In particular, two key questions are raised. First, what challenges can be identified which face any future developments within environmental policy and what direction might one expect it to take? Secondly, a more fundamental question concerns the ideological nature of green politics and the EU. Given the issues raised throughout this book, is it possible to identify the EU as an effective channel for the implementation of green political ideas? Is there a true commitment from EU member states and institutions to tackle environmental problems fully, or are green issues a side issue when compared to the dynamics of the single European market?

The Progress of Environmental Policy

Undoubtedly progress has clearly been made in the field of EU environmental legislation. On quantitative grounds one would have to admit that the requirements placed upon EU member states to maintain broad environmental standards has rapidly expanded. From no legal competence in the Treaty of Rome, the EU now has competence in a full range of environmental policies, covering policy spheres with a broad diversity, from issues concerning water pollution to car recycling. The aims and objectives of the fifth and sixth EAPs, for example, are far more advanced than the early initial steps within the environmental field. The EU itself has moved away from relying upon interpretation of legislation to a commitment to a sustainable union. For example, Article 3c now states that:

Environmental protection requirements must be integrated into the
definition and implementation of Community policies and activities ...
in particular with a view to promoting sustainable development.

The EEB noted that this commitment was a 'radical change of course
after forty years of placing economic growth at the top of the EC's
political priorities' (in Connelly and Smith, 1999: 241).

The expansion of EC policy competence has without doubt produced
some significant, practical environmental achievements. These include
reducing CO_2 and other greenhouse gas emissions by 2.5% between
1990 and 1998, cutting emissions of sulphur dioxide by 50% between
1980–95, and there have also been marked declines in the amounts of
lead and mercury in the atmosphere (EEA 1998). The competence of
the EU to act in this area is rarely questioned and indeed it appears that
there is a growing consensus that the EU level is, perhaps, the best level
to tackle issues that 'know no borders'. DG Environment and many
environmental actors would argue, however, that there are still major
problems that need to be overcome, especially in terms of how policy is
made. The integrative nature of the environment means that it needs to
be tackled across policy areas. Despite reference to this in the Treaties
and the various Action Programmes very little has been done to fully
integrate the environment into all relevant policy areas. This was partly
due to the attitude within the Commission that the environment was
'voguish' and also the desire to protect bureaucratic competencies.
These factors meant that at first environmental problems were not taken
as seriously as other issues within the Commission. When the issue was
finally taken seriously, bureaucrats in other DGs were not happy having
DG Environment snooping around checking up on how well they were
integrating the environment into their activities.

However, as the previous chapters demonstrate, these problems are
also exacerbated by a lack of political will on behalf of some of the
member states, which has been reflected in the poor levels of implementation of some EU environmental legislation. This places an important emphasis upon the role of environmental campaigners to act as
watchdogs on member states and to ensure their compliance to environmental legislation. There is also reluctance on the part of member states
to give up unanimity in the Council for the so-called 'red-line' issues
such as tax, which again remained off the agenda at the Nice Summit.
While such issues remain a significant stumbling block, the integration
of environmental concerns throughout relevant EU policy areas will

continue to be sporadic. Although the fifth EAP made belated attempts to tackle the problem of integration, its ability to push through reforms have also been hampered by the lack of EU competence in two of the five key areas identified by the programme: energy and tourism. Clearly, therefore, there is still broad scope for future development. The sixth EAP acknowledges that it alone cannot achieve the results needed, but by highlighting the issues and problems that continue to threaten the European environment and where EU actions have not had the desired result, it can help move the EU another step closer to the aim of a sustainable society.

A Changing Environmental Discourse?

Some of the problems outlined above undoubtedly reflect the diverse attitudes towards the importance of environmental policy making and the direction in which it should be steered. It has been clear throughout this discussion that opinions vary dramatically from those environmental supporters, such as the green actors discussed in Chapter 4, who claim that current EU environmental legislation only scratches the surface of the problem, to those 'laggard' member states who, for a variety of reasons, are reluctant to agree to, or indeed implement, stricter environmental standards. In between these two poles lie all those actors who recognize the importance of the environmental problem, yet differ over the approach to environmental protection and the types of policy best suited to achieving effective results. The development of EU environmental policy has without doubt reflected this diversity of opinion throughout its history.

Chapter 2 highlighted the broad debates and divisions prevalent within environmental politics regarding what was needed to protect and maintain the condition of the environment. It is evident from the subsequent chapters that many of these debates have largely been mirrored within the EU policy-making process. As such, when trying to assess the progress of environmental awareness and change at this level, the question of a transition in discourse is a significant aspect to any assessment.

Utilizing the categories developed by Dryzek as a guide, one can identify an interesting transition in the style of environmental discourse present within the EU. A broader understanding and awareness of the environmental sphere has evolved within the EU policy-making process. Connelly and Smith similarly adopt this stance, arguing that the acceptance by the EU, after much debate, of the concept of 'sustainable development' marks the primary focal point of this change (Connelly and Smith 1999: 241). As Chapter 3 demonstrated, the recognition of the need for a more sustainable approach to economic and societal development is important here as it marks a shift in attitude by the EU away from the largely reactive, problem-solving discourse upon which its earlier attempts at environmental policy-making were structured.

This new approach was evident within the EU's commitment to the Agenda 21 principles, which the EU signed up to in Rio in 1992. As Chapter 5 demonstrated, it was also a significant part of the rationale behind the development of the fifth and sixth EAPs, which sought to move away from a focus upon short-term, 'quick fix' solutions towards developing more long-term, sustainable standards. While many green activists may view this process sceptically and see the EU's interpretation as a very 'weak' form of sustainability, it nevertheless represents a significant marker in the EU's environmental development. On the one hand, these principles arguably reflect an increasing role for green ideas and an awareness of the broader environmental discourse within the EU institutions. More practically, it commits the EU to a wider interpretation of environmental issues.

Unsurprisingly, as the author of these EAPs, DG Environment is very supportive of this discourse, even though taken to its logical conclusion it could potentially mark the beginning of the end for the DG itself. However, DG Environment's enthusiastic support must be tempered by the reactions from those less supportive of such approaches. The main stumbling block comes from other DGs, who appear wedded to a distinctly neo-liberal attitude. Changing the attitudes and discourses of these DGs is a far greater, and realistically more distant, challenge than that presented by altering the views of DG Environment. To this end, the current weakness of the Integration Unit as an agent of change represents a major concern for members of DG Environment.

While it may be impossible to identify a direct correlation between the greater influence of social agents upon the environmental agenda and a reshaping of the environmental discourse within the EU, it appears that these groups have been able to have some impact upon the process. However, again one must be wary of identifying this as a radical shift in EU policy making. As mentioned, although DG

Environment in particular may have adopted a broader environmental discourse, it is harder to identify the same process across all Commission DGs. Beyond this small 'environmental haven' it would appear that more traditional economic and industrial perspectives continue to predominate. While stricter environmental controls may be emerging, the pressure still remains upon the environmental campaigners to justify why change is needed and pollution prevented, rather than on the polluters to justify why existing methods should be continued and current pollution levels maintained. This imbalance is further reflected by the reliance upon campaigners to act as 'watchdogs' and enforce compliance upon member states to EU environmental regulations.

For green actors, however, all is not lost. There is also sympathy for the sustainability discourse within the EP, an institution often receptive to the views of the environmental movement. The increased use of co-decision as a result of the Treaty of Amsterdam raises the possibility of this discourse having a stronger input into the direction of EU environmental policy. In addition, there is also evidence of changing attitudes towards the environmental discourse from among a number of influential member states. Recent years have witnessed an increase in support for green parties at both European and national level. The emergence of green parties within member state governments therefore, represents an important new channel of influence and pressure. Indeed, the reluctance of countries such as France, Germany, Sweden and Finland to sign up to the compromise emissions deal, brokered by John Prescott between the EU and the USA at the end of the Hague Climate Change Summit in November 2000, marks a significant departure away from the 'any deal is a success' mentality often previously evident at such meetings, and was clearly influenced by the participation of green representatives such as Dominique Voynet.

The Hague Summit debacle also highlights another future obstacle for a 'greener' EU. If the global environmental crisis is as severe as many reports suggest, getting the EU's house in order on environmental issues represents only one part of the overall conundrum. It was stated earlier that one of the principle reasons behind EU action on the environment was the fact that environmental problems 'know no borders', and that it was not enough for an individual state to implement green policies if they were subject to other countries' continued pollution. The same argument can also be applied to the EU. It is not enough for the EU to improve environmental standards if other nations throughout the world continue to increase the damage inflicted upon the environment. Hence, while improving EU environmental policies may be a step in the right direction, just tackling these issues within EU borders may not be enough.

The need for global action is paramount. While, the role of the EU as a global green actor has been explored more fully elsewhere (Bretherton and Vogler 1999), both the Rio and Kyoto Summits highlighted the benefits of EU states working together in an attempt to tackle global environmental problems. It would, therefore, be potentially advantageous to grant the Commission similar powers in the 'Earth Summits' as it has in World Trade Organization talks. The EU 'speaking with one voice' could facilitate burden-sharing within the EU and may even increase the pressure upon countries like the USA to 'green' their economies and ways of life. To achieve this level of impact, however, the EU needs to integrate its sustainability discourse into many additional areas of policy competence. These would include its aid and development programmes, the Lomé conventions and so on. The realistic prospects of the EU being ready to adopt this role, however, was significantly damaged after the Hague meetings with the 'leader/ laggard' divisions again strongly in evidence. This situation is almost certain to be exacerbated by any process of enlargement within the EU. Although the enlargement process, especially Agenda 2000, includes the environmental *acquis*, enlargement would almost certainly tip the current dynamic in favour of the 'laggards', making a distant prospect for truly effective international green action even more unlikely.

A Future for Green Politics at the EU level?

How, then, can one summarize the environmental achievements of the EU and what might the future hold in store for green politics at EU level? Overall, this book has identified significant progress within environmental policy making within the EU, and suggested a potential shift in the discourse surrounding green issues. However, it has also shown that the changes identified fall some way short of being what one could truly identify as a 'greening' of the EU.

Significant challenges and barriers still confront the claims of those who seek to identify the EU as a key green actor. At a relatively simplistic level, the fact that the EU has gone from an organization focused almost entirely upon the promotion of economic growth and prosperity with no specific commitment to the environment, to an initiator of environmental standards and legislation represents a distinct improvement in its environmental credentials. While the changes that have taken place may not necessarily represent the type of green politics that some would wish to see, the EU's attitudes towards the environment have come a long way, and organizations such as the EEA are stridently pushing for more. Its own summary of the EU's environmental achievements represents a suitable 'mid-term report':

> The EU is making progress in reducing certain pressures on the environment, though this is not enough to improve the general quality of the environment and even less to progress to sustainability. Without accelerated policies, pressures on the environment will continue to exceed human health standards and the often limited carrying capacity of the environment (in Collier 1997: 2).

Overall then, it appears that a general assessment would read 'tries hard but could do better'. Undoubtedly, environmental issues will continue to be a key area of policy development within the EU. Additionally, it is an area that will face increasing pressures with the prospect of EU enlargement and the admission of countries from Eastern Europe who possess lower environmental standards. This process will undoubtedly place significant strain upon the current legislation, both regarding its adequacy and the ability of the EU to enforce it. Clearly, there is the potential that environmental issues may be forced to take a back-seat to other more pressing issues which enlargement may bring. However, these concerns may also provide a focal point for further debate regarding green politics within the EU.

Bibliography

Arp, H.
1992   'The European Parliament in EC Environmental Policy', European Union Institute Working Paper 92.13 (Florence: EUI).

Baker, S.
1996   'Environmental Policy in the European Union: Institutional Dilemmas and Democratic Practice', in M. Lafferty and J. Meadowcroft (eds.), *Democracy and the Environment* (Aldershot: Edward Elgar): 213-23.
1997   'The Evolution of EU Environmental Policy: From Growth to Sustainable Development?' in S. Baker, M. Kousis, D. Richardson and S. Young (eds.), *The Politics of Sustainable Development: Theory, Policy and Practice within the EU* (London: Routledge): 91-106.

Baker, S., M. Kousis, D. Richardson and S. Young
1997   'Introduction: The Theory and Practice of Sustainable Development in EU Perspective', in *idem*, *The Politics of Sustainable Development: Theory, Policy and Practice within the EU* (London: Routledge): 1-40.

Barnes, P., and I. Barnes
1999   *Environmental Policy in the EU* (Cheltenham: Edward Elgar).

Barry, J.
1994   'The Limits of the Shallow and the Deep: Green Politics, Philosophy, and Praxis, *Environmental Politics,* 3.3: 369-94.

Bomberg, E.
1996   'Greens in the European Parliament', *Environmental Politics* 5.2: 324-31.
1998   *Green Parties and Politics in the EU* (London: Routledge).

Borzel, T.A.
2000   'Why There Is No "Southern Problem": On Environmental Leaders and Laggards in the EU', *Journal of European Public Policy* 7.1: 141-62.

Bretherton, C., and J. Vogler
1999   *Europe as a Global Actor* (London: Routledge).

Brundtland, G.H.
1987   *Our Common Future: The Report of the World Commission on Environment and Development* (Oxford: Oxford University Press).

Bulmer, S.
1994   'Institutions and Policy Change in the EC', *Public Administration*, 72.3: 423-44.

Burchell, J.
1996   'No to the EU: The Swedish Green Party's Performance in the 1995 European Parliamentary Elections', *Environmental Politics*, 5.2: 331-37.

Burchell, J.
      2000   'Here Come the Greens (again): The Green Party in Britain during the
                    1990s', *Environmental Politics*, 9.3: 145-50.
Butt Philip, A.
      1998   'The EU: Environmental Policy and the Prospects for Sustainable
                    Development', in K. Hanf and A. Jansen (eds.), *Governance and
                    Environment in Western Europe* (Harlow: Longman): 253-76.
Carson, R.
      1965   *The Silent Spring* (Harmondsworth: Penguin Books).
Carter, N.
      1994   'The Greens in the 1994 European Parliament Elections' *Environmental
                    Politics* 3: 445-517.
CEC (Commission of the European Communities)
      1992   *Towards Sustainability: A Community Programme of Policy and Action
                    in Relation to the Environment* (Fifth Environmental Action Programme)
                    COM (92) 23, 27 March.
      1996   'Progress Report from the Commission on the Implementation of the
                    Community Programme of Policy and Action Relating to the Environ-
                    ment and Sustainable Development', COM (95) 624, Brussels.
      1997   *The EU and the Environment* (Luxembourg: CEC).
Christie, I.
      1999   *Sustaining Europe: A Common Cause for the EU in the New Century*
                    (London: Demos/Green Alliance).
Church, C., and D. Phinnemore
      1994   *European Union and European Community: A Handbook and Commen-
                    tary on the 1992 Maastricht Treaties* (London: Prentice Hall).
Cichowski, R.
      1998   'Integrating the Environment: the European Court and the Construction of
                    Supranational Policy', *Journal of European Public Policy* 5.3: 387-405.
Collier, U.
      1997   'Sustainability, Subsidiarity and Deregulation', *Environmental Politics*
                    6.2: 1-23.
Collier, U., and J. Golub
      1997   'Environmental Policy and Politics', in M. Rhodes, P. Heywood and V.
                    Wright (eds.), *Developments in West European Politics* (Basingstoke:
                    Macmillan): 226-43.
Collins, K., and D. Earnshaw
      1993   'The Implementation and Enforcement of EC Environment Legislation'
                    in D. Judge (ed.), *A Green Dimension for the EC* (London: Frank Cass):
                    213-49.
Connelly, J., and G. Smith
      1999   *Politics and the Environment: From Theory to Practice* (London:
                    Routledge).
Cram, L.
      1996   'Integration Theory and the Study of the European Policy Process' in J.
                    Richardson (ed.), *European Union: Power and Policy-Making* (London:
                    Routledge): 40-58.

Dalton, R.J.
    1993   'The Environmental Movement in Western Europe.' in S. Kamieniecki (ed.), *Environmental Politics in the International Arena: Movements, Parties, Organisations and Policy* (New York: State University of New York Press): 41-68.
    1994   *The Green Rainbow: Environmental Groups in Western Europe* (New Haven: Yale University Press).

David, H.
    1994   'A Long Way', in *EEB Twentieth Anniversary* (EEB Homepage).

DG Environment
    www.europa.eu.int/comm/dgs/environment/index_en.htm

Dobson, A.
    1990   *Green Political Thought* (London: Unwin Hyman).
    1995   *Green Political Thought* (London: Routledge, 2nd edn).

Doherty, B.
    1992   'The Fundi-Realo Controversy: An Analysis of Four European Green Parties', *Environmental Politics* 1.1: 95-120.

Dryzek, J.S.
    1997   *The Politics of the Earth: Environmental Discourses* (Oxford: Oxford University Press).

Eckersley, R.
    1992   *Environmentalism and Political Theory: Towards an Ecocentric Approach* (London: UCL Press).

European Environment Agency
    1996   *Environmental Taxes: Implementation and Environmental Effectiveness. EEA Environmental Issues Series No. 1* (Copenhagen: European Environment Agency).
    1998   *Europe's Environment: The Second Assessment. Data Pocketbook* (Luxembourg: European Environment Agency).

European Environmental Bureau
    www.eeb.org

Environment for Europeans
    Magazine of DG Environment, various issues, Brussels.

European Policy Centre
    www.theepc.be

Eur-op News
    2000   Environment Supplement to Eur-op News 2.

Francis, A.
    1999   'Environmental Issues in CEEC Transformation', in M. Mannin (ed.), *Pushing Back the Boundaries* (Manchester: Manchester University Press): 158-82.

Frankland, G., and D. Schoonmaker
    1992   *Between Protest and Power: The Green Party in Germany* (Boulder, CO: Westview Press).

Freestone, D.
    1991   'European Community Environmental Policy and Law', *Journal of Law and Society* 18: 135-54.

Golub, J.
    1996   'Sovereignty and Subsidiarity in EU Environmental Policy', *Political Studies* 4.44: 686-703.
    1998   'New Instruments for Environmental Policy in the EU: An Overview', European Union Institute Working Paper, No. 98/12, Florence.
Grant, W.
    1993   'Transnational Companies and Environmental Policy Making: The Trend of Globalization' in J.D. Liefferink, P. Lowe and A. Mol (eds.), *European Integration and Environmental Policy* (London: Belhaven): 59-74.
Greenwood, J.
    1997   *Representing Interests in the EU* (Basingstoke: Macmillan).
Hagland, P.
    1991   'Environmental Policy' in L. Hurwitz and C. Lequesne (eds.), *The State of the European Community: Policies, Institutions and Debates in the Transition Years* (Boulder, CO: Lynne Rienner): 258-81.
Haigh, N.
    1989   *EEC Environmental Policy and Britain* (Harlow: Longman).
    1999   'EU Environment Policy at 25: Retrospect and Prospect' *Environment and Planning C: Government and Policy* 17: 109-12.
Hardin, G.
    1968   'The Tragedy of the Commons', *Science* 162: 1243-48.
Hildebrand, P.
    1993   'The EC's Environmental Policy, 1957 to "1992": From Incidental Measures to an International Regime?' in D. Judge (ed.), *A Green Dimension for the EC* (London: Frank Cass): 13-44.
Hix, S.
    1999   *The Political System of the EU* (Basingstoke: Macmillan).
Jacobs, M.
    1997   'Introduction: The New Politics of the Environment' in M. Jacobs (ed.), *Greening the Millennium?* (Oxford: Basil Blackwell): 1-17.
Jordan, A.
    1999a   'Editorial Introduction: The Construction of a Multilevel Environment Governance System' *Environment and Planning C: Government and Policy* 17: 1-17.
    1999b   'The Implementation of EU Environmental Policy' *Environment and Planning C: Government and Policy* 17: 69-90.
Judge, D.
    1993   'A Green Dimension for the EC' in D. Judge (ed.), *A Green Dimension for the EC* (London: Frank Cass): 1-9.
Kenny, M.
    1994   'Ecologism', in R. Eccleshall, V. Geoghegan, R. Jay, M. Kenny, I. McKenzie and R. Wilford (eds.), *Political Ideologies: An Introduction* (London: Routledge, 2nd edn): 218-51.
Kitschelt, H.
    1988   'Left Libertarian Parties: Explaining Innovation in Competitive Party Systems', *World Politics* 40.2: 194-234.
    1993   'The Green Phenomenon in Western Party Systems', in S. Kamieniecki (ed.), *Environmental Politics in the International Arena: Movements,*

Parties, Organisations and Policy (New York: State University of New York Press): 93-112.

Labour Party
1995   *The Future of the European Union: Report on Labour's Position in Preparation for the IGC 1996* (London: Labour Party).

Lenschow, A.
1999   'The Greening of the EU: The CAP and the Structural Funds', *Environment and Planning C: Government and Policy* 17: 91-108.

Liberatore, A.
1991   'The Problems of Transnational Policy-Making: Environmental Policy in the EC', *European Journal of Political Research* 19.2-3: 281-305.
1997   'The Integration of Sustainable Development Objectives into EU Policy-making' in S. Baker, M. Kousis, D. Richardson and S. Young (eds.), *The Politics of Sustainable Development: Theory, Policy and Practice within the EU* (London: Routledge): 107-26.

Liefferink, D.
1997   'The Netherlands: A Net Exporter of Environmental Policy Concepts', in M.S. Andersen and D. Liefferink (eds.), *European Environmental Policy. The Pioneers* (Manchester: Manchester University Press).

Liefferink, D., and M.S. Anderson
1998   'Strategies of the "Green" Member States in EU Environmental Policy-making', *Journal of European Public Policy*, 5.2: 254-70.

Liefferink, D., P. Lowe and A. Mol
1993   'Introduction' in *idem* (eds.), *European Integration and Environmental Policy* (London: Belhaven): 1-14.

Lightfoot, S., and D. Luckin
2000   'The 1999 Ecological Tax Reform Law', *German Politics*, 9.1: 139-44.

Lodge, J.
1989   'Environment: Towards a Clean Blue-green EC?' in *idem* (ed.), *The European Community and the Challenge of the Future* (London: Pinter): 319-26.

Long, T.
1998   'The Environmental Lobby' in P. Lowe and S. Ward (eds.), *British Environmental Policy and Europe: Politics and Policy in Transition* (London: Routledge): 105-18.

Lowe, P., and J. Goyder
1983   *Environmental Groups in Politics* (London: George Allen & Unwin)

Lowe, P., and S. Ward (eds.)
1998   *British Environmental Policy and Europe: Politics and Policy in Transition* (London: Routledge).

Lucas, C.
2001   'Free Market Europe: A Growing Threat to the Environment', *The Ecologist* March.

Luckin, D., and S. Lightfoot
1999   'Environmental Taxation in Contemporary European Politics', *Contemporary Politics* 5.3: 243-61.

Majone, G.
    1994   'The Rise of the Regulatory State in Europe' *West European Politics*
                17.3: 77-101.
Markovits, A., and P. Gorski
    1993   *The German Left: Red, Green and Beyond* (New York: Oxford University
                Press).
Marks, G., and D. McAdam
    1996   'Social Movements and the Changing Structure of Political Opportunity
                in the European Union', *West European Politics* 19.2: 249-78.
Mazey, S., and J. Richardson
    1992   'Environmental Groups and the EC: Challenges and Opportunities',
                Environmental Politics 1.4: 109-28.
    1993   *Lobbying in the European Community* (Oxford: Oxford University Press).
McCormick, J.
    1991   *British Politics and the Environment* (London: Earthscan).
    1999   'Environmental Policy', in L. Cram, D. Dinan and N. Nugent (eds.),
                Developments in the EU (Basingstoke: Macmillan): 193-210.
Meadows, D.H., D.L. Meadows, J. Randers and W.W. Behrens
    1972   *The Limits to Growth* (London: Pan).
Merchant, C.
    1992   *Radical Ecology: The Search for a Liveable World* (London: Routledge).
Morata, F., and N. Font
    1998   'Spain: Environmental Policy and Public Administration. A Marriage of
                Convenience Officiated by the EU?', in K. Hanf and A. Jansen (eds.),
                Governance and Environment in Western Europe (Harlow: Longman):
                208-29.
Müller-Rommel, F.
    1989   *New Politics in Western Europe: The Rise and Success of Green Parties
                and Alternative Lists* (Boulder, CO: Westview Press).
Naess, A.
    1973   'The Shallow and the Deep, Long Range Ecology Movement: A
                Summary', *Inquiry* 16: 265-70.
Peterson, J.
    1995   'Playing the Transparency Game: Policy-making and Consultation in the
                European Commission', *Public Administration* 73: 473-92.
Peterson, J., and E. Bomberg
    1999   *Decision-Making in the EU* (Basingstoke: Macmillan).
Poguntke, T.
    1987   'New Politics and Party Systems: The Emergence of a New Type of
                Party?', *West European Politics* 10.1: 76-88.
Pollack, M.
    2000   'The End of Creeping Competence? EU Policy-making Since Maastricht',
                Journal of Common Market Studies, 38.3: 519-38.
Rosamond, B.
    2000   *Theories of European Integration* (London: Palgrave).
Rucht, D.
    1993   'Think Globally, Act Locally? Needs, Forms and Problems of Cross-
                national Co-operation among Environmental Groups', in J.D. Liefferink,

P. Lowe and A. Mol (eds.), *European Integration and Environmental Policy* (London: Belhaven): 75-95.

Sbragia, A.
1996   'Environmental Policy' in H. Wallace and W. Wallace (eds.), *Policy Making in the EU* (Oxford: Oxford University Press, 3rd edn): 235-57.
2000   'Environmental Policy' in H. Wallace and W. Wallace (eds.), *Policy Making in the EU* (Oxford: Oxford University Press, 4th edn): 293-316.

Schlegelmilch, K.
1998   *Energy Taxation in the EU and some Member States: Looking for Opportunities Ahead* (Wuppertal Institute for Climate, Environment and Energy: Science Centre North Rhine-Westphalia).

Vincent, A.
1992   *Modern Political Ideologies* (Oxford: Basil Blackwell).
1993   'The Character of Ecology', *Environmental Politics* 2.2: 248-76.

Vogel, D.
1993   'The Making of EC Environmental Policy', in S. Andersen and K. Eliassen (eds.), *Making Policy in Europe* (London: Sage): 115-32.
1997   'Trading Up and Governing Across: Transnational Governance and Environmental Protection', *Journal of European Public Policy* 4.4: 556-71

Weale, A.
1996   'Environmental Rules and Rule-making in the EU' *Journal of European Public Policy* 3.4: 594-611.
1999   'European Environmental Policy by Stealth?' *Environment and Planning C: Government and Policy* 17: 37-51.

Weale, A., and A. Williams
1993   'Between Economy and Ecology? The Single Market and the Integration of Environmental Policy' in D. Judge (ed.), *A Green Dimension for the EC* (London: Frank Cass): 45-64.

Wilkinson, D.
1997   'Towards Sustainability in the EU? Steps within the European Commission towards Integrating the Environment into other EU Policy Sectors', *Environmental Politics* 6.1: 153-73.

Wurzel, R.
1993   'Environmental Policy' in J. Lodge (ed.), *The European Community and the Challenge of the Future* (London: Pinter, 2nd edn): 178-99.

Wynne, B. and C. Waterton
1998   *British Environmental Policy and Europe: Politics and Policy in Transition* (London: Routledge).

General Index

Index of Authors

UNIVERSITY ASSOCIATION FOR CONTEMPORARY EUROPEAN STUDIES
UACES Secretariat, King's College London, Strand, London WC2R 2LS, UK
Tel: +44 (0)20 7240 0206   Fax: +44 (0)20 7836 2350   Email: admin@uaces.org
www.uaces.org

UACES

★ UACES ★

University Association for Contemporary European Studies

The Association
- Brings together academics involved in researching Europe with representatives of government, industry and the media who are active in European affairs
- Primary organisation for British academics researching the European Union
- Over 600 individual and corporate members from Dept such as Politics, Law, Economics & European Studies, plus over 150 Graduate Students who join as Associate Members

Membership Benefits
- Individual Members eligible for special highly reduced fee for The Journal of Common Market Studies (JCMS)
- Regular Newsletter - events and developments of relevance to members
- Conferences - variety of themes, modestly priced, further reductions for members
- Publications, including the new series *Contemporary European Studies*, launched in 1998
- Research Network, and research conference
- Through the European Community Studies Association (ECSA), access to a larger world wide network
- Information Documentation & Resources eg: The Register of Courses in European Studies and the Register of Research into European Integration

Current Cost of Membership per annum
Individual Members: £25.00   Associate (Student): £10.00   Corporate Members: £50.00

APPLICATION FOR MEMBERSHIP OF UACES
Please complete the appropriate details and return the entire form to the address above.

Last Name: _____   First Name: _____ Title (eg Mr): ____

Institution: _____

Faculty / Dept: _____

Institution Address: _____

_____

Work Tel No: _____   Work Fax No: _____

Home Tel No: _____   Home Fax No: _____

E-mail: _____

Address for correspondence if different: _____

_____

Where did you hear about UACES? _____

Signature and Date: _____

PTO TO COMPLETE PAYMENT DETAILS

CES Ad1

UNIVERSITY ASSOCIATION FOR CONTEMPORARY EUROPEAN STUDIES
UACES Secretariat, King's College London, Strand, London WC2R 2LS, UK
Tel: +44 (0)20 7240 0206   Fax: +44 (0)20 7836 2350   Email: admin@uaces.org
www.uaces.org

PAYMENT DETAILS

TO PAY BY CHEQUE*

I wish to pay my membership subscription by cheque. Please make cheques payable to UACES, not King's College.

Please find enclosed a cheque (in pounds sterling) for:
£25 (Individual)   £10 (Associate - Student)   £50 (Corporate)

* Please Note: we are no longer able to accept Eurocheques

TO PAY BY CREDIT/DEBIT CARD

I wish to pay my membership subscription by (mark appropriate box):
Visa   Mastercard   Eurocard   Switch Solo

I authorise you to debit my Account with the amount of (mark appropriate box):
£25 (Individual)   £10 (Associate - Student)   £50 (Corporate)

Signature of cardholder: _____   Date: _____

My Card Number is: □□□□ □□□□ □□□□ □□□□ □□□

Cardholder's Name and Initials*:_____ Cardholder's Title* (eg Mr): _____
*As shown on the card

Expiry Date: □□□   Start Date (if present*): □□□   Issue No. (if present*): □
*Usually for Switch and Solo cards

Cardholder's address and postcode (if different from overleaf):
_____

TO PAY BY STANDING ORDER* (UK Bank only)
*This option not available for Corporate or Associate (Student) members

Please complete the details below and return to UACES. We will process the membership application and then forward this authority to your bank. This authority is not a Direct Debit authority (ie we cannot take money out of your bank account without your permission).

To (insert your Bank Name) _____ at (insert your bank address)
_____
_____ (insert Post Code) _____, UK.

Please pay to Lloyds Bank, Pall Mall Branch, 8-10 Waterloo Place, London SW1Y 4BE, UK, in favour of UACES, Account No. 3781242, Sort-Code 30-00-08, on the (insert date, eg 1st) _____ day of (insert month, eg June) _____ , the sum of £25 (TWENTY FIVE POUNDS) and the same sum on the same date each year until countermanded.

Signature: _____   Date: _____
Name: _____
Address: _____
Account No.: _____   Sort-code: _____

CES Ad1